Books by Albert Camus

Awarded the Nobel Prize for Literature in 1957

Youthful
Writings

"Cahiers II"

The First Camus

An Introductory Essay by

Paul Viallaneix

Youthful Writings

by Albert Camus

Translated from the French by

Ellen Conroy Kennedy

 Paragon House, *New York*

First Paragon House edition, 1990

Published in the United States by

Paragon House
90 Fifth Avenue
New York, NY 10011

Published by arrangement with Alfred A. Knopf, Inc.
Originally published in France as *Cahiers Albert
Camus 2: Le Premier Camus* by Gallimard, Paris.
Copyright © 1973 by Éditions Gallimard.

10 9 8 7 6 5 4 3 2 1

Library of Congress Cataloging-in-Publication Data

Camus, Albert, 1913–1960.
    [Écrits de jeunesse. English]
    The first Camus / by Albert Camus; translated
from the French by Ellen Conroy Kennedy. — 1st
Paragon House ed.
        p.   cm.
    At head of title: The first Camus, an introductory
essay by Paul Viallaneix.
    Translation of: Écrits de jeunesse.
    ISBN 1-55778-387-X
    1. Camus, Albert, 1913–1960—Translations,
English.   I. Title.
    [PQ2605.A3734E2513   1990]
    848'.91409—dc20   90-30210
                                             CIP

This book is printed on acid-free paper.
Manufactured in the United States of America

Contents

The First Camus
by Paul Viallaneix

Youthful Writings
by Albert Camus

1932

Contents

The First Camus

by Paul Viallaneix

Chapter I

The First
Man

> Death and a writer's work. Just be-
> fore dying, he has his last work read
> over to him. He still hasn't said what
> he had to say. He orders it to be
> burned. And he dies with nothing to
> console him—and with something
> snapping in his heart like a broken
> chord.   December, 1938
> —*Notebooks 1935–1942*, p. 108

As a young man, Camus did not intend to become a
militant writer.* Yet the success of his early works in
France was due to historical circumstance. Amid the
night and fog of Nazi oppression, the final act of faith in
The Myth of Sisyphus roused a fragile but salutary gleam
of hope: "The struggle itself . . . is enough to fill a
human heart. One must imagine Sisyphus happy" (p.
123). The young people who resolved then to "resist"

---

* The mistrust committed writings inspired in Camus was evident
not only in his attitude as a young writer. He expressed it several
times in *Alger Républicain*. About Paul Nizan's *La Conspiration*,
he wrote on November 11, 1938: "For some years party membership has been much discussed and written of. But, all things considered, it's a problem as futile as that of immortality, an affair
each man must settle for himself and on which others should not
pass judgment. One joins the party the way one gets married.
And where a writer is concerned, it's in his work that one can
judge the effect of his beliefs" (*Essais*, p. 1396). Or again, writing
of Ignazio Silone's novel *Bread and Wine:* "I believe that if our
time teaches us anything on this score, it is that a revolutionary
art, if it is not to lapse into the basest forms of expression, cannot
do without artistic importance" (*Lyrical and Critical Essays*,
p. 208). [P.V.]

3

the established order, like others since who have chosen to "fight the system," drew their inspiration from this *sursum corda*. Then there was *Caligula*. The vanquished hero's farewell, shouted out by the voice of Gérard Philipe, cast a garish light upon that year of disgrace, 1945, which the discovery of the death camps, the bloody rioting at Sétif,* and the hecatomb at Hiroshima had just, with Europe scarcely liberated, dishonored: "My freedom isn't the right one. . . . Oh, how oppressive is this darkness! . . . We shall be forever guilty. The air tonight is heavy as the sum of human sorrows" (*Caligula and Three Other Plays*, p. 73).

The horrors of war gave way to postwar violence, not all of it merely verbal. Camus's early literary work had been conceived in Algeria during the last years of peace. (A completed manuscript of *Caligula* addressed to Jean Paulhan dates from 1939; *The Stranger* was finished in May, 1940; the first part of *The Myth of Sisyphus* in September. Camus had been working on *Caligula* since January, 1937, and on *The Stranger* since May of 1938.) Later, as editorial writer for *Combat*,† his journalistic work having brought him to Paris, he felt he must develop what his work had given him occasion to witness during the Occupation. Most of his readers appreciated his courage. Others, more and more numerous in the Paris intelligentsia, made fun of his obstinacy. They had all got in the habit of expecting from him the maxim of the day. This is why they threw themselves upon *The Plague* as if it were a fable, with the expectation of discovering a moral in it, rather than assessing the effort the author of *The Stranger* had made to renew his narrative style and to transpose the experience of the Occupation into a work of art.

* In Algeria. [E.C.K.]

† The underground newspaper. [E.C.K.]

4

In publishing *The Rebel*, Camus aggravated the misunderstanding that was alienating him from his admirers as well as from his adversaries. Inadvertently he gave credence to an error Sartre had been the first to commit, of looking upon *The Stranger* as a fictional illustration of the thinking in *The Myth of Sisyphus*.* From that moment on, an out-and-out attack against Camus's "philosophy" seemed to devaluate his literary work. Given the weaknesses of one, people hastened to conclude that the other was outmoded. Disgusted at first, Camus reacted against the attacks he had been subjected to. *Exile and the Kingdom, The Fall*, certain of his works for the theater, like his admirable adaptation of Faulkner's *Requiem for a Nun*, mark the stages of his return to literature. At Stockholm, in his Nobel Prize acceptance speech, Camus described himself as an "artist." This was the first term he used to describe himself (*Essais*, p. 1072). He did not regard himself as a moralist, still less as one of those professors of ethics whose hypocrisy Clamence in *The Fall* would inherit and expose to ridicule. But it was too late, or too early, for the accused man to exonerate himself once and for all. Even his fame served him ill. It had made him into a personality with whom he, too, had to reckon. In the expectation of other books that would one day restore his status as first and foremost a writer, it was difficult for him to endure the lack of understanding he was faced with. When asked this kind of question: "What do you believe French critics have neglected in your work?" he would answer impatiently, "The dark part, that which is blind and instinctive in it. French critics are interested above all in ideas" (last interview with Camus, December 20, 1959,

---

* See Jean-Paul Sartre's *An Explication of "The Stranger"* in *Camus: A Collection of Critical Essays*, Germaine Brée, ed. (New York: Prentice-Hall, 1962), pp. 108–121. [E.C.K.]

Essais, p. 1925). Perhaps recalling the fate of Meursault, Camus had already been wondering for a long time how to go about reestablishing the truth, *his* truth. In one of his unpublished *Notebooks*, at the time of his quarrel with Sartre, Camus noted: "Who will bear witness for us? Our work. Alas! What else? No one, no one except . . . those who love us. . . . But love is silence: each man dies unknown." He did in fact die "unknown," like Jan in *The Misunderstanding*, from not having known or wished to spell out his identity at the appropriate moment.

Today it seems less difficult to approach the real Camus. A whole new generation reads him without caring about the role that circumstance once assigned him, almost despite himself. His work has become classical—not, as used to happen, with time, but because of its rapid diffusion throughout the world. This classical quality protected his work from the passions of his own historical moment, which, once having served him well, might have relegated him to the category of has-been. Translated into more than twenty languages (one can get an idea of their number and diversity from Roger Quilliot's bibliography, which follows Camus's *Essais* in the French Pléiade edition), welcomed into the most diverse cultures, Camus's work has ceased to belong to the French generation of which it was the conscience. Camus will not be a second Jules Romains, or another Martin du Gard.*

If there is any doubt, reconsider the evidence. *The*

---

* Two writers who were extremely popular in France between the two world wars but are very little read today. [E.C.K.]

Did Camus imagine his literary destiny might one day be compared to Roger Martin du Gard's? Camus admired *Les Thibault*, thought *Jean Barois* "the only great novel of the age of scientism," and considered that their author, "a just and forgiving man," would remain "our perpetual contemporary." See *Roger Martin du Gard* in *Lyrical . . . Essays*, pp. 254–287. [P.V.]

Stranger remains an enigma. No interpretation, however minutely detailed, has drawn out all its meaning. *The Plague* reveals the complexity of Camus's heroes. Who is Tarrou? Who is Rieux? Who is Grand? Who is Cottard? Readers have often very wrongly taken Tarrou's formula "to be a saint without God" as a password. One must restore it to the context of the novel (*The Plague*, p. 230). He who would define these characters by whatever formula one or another of them might pronounce is either very clever or very foolhardy. Their silhouettes, immobilized beneath the light of a reality that had been scorching, tremble henceforth in the haze of their fictional existence. *State of Siege* awaits some more fortunate producer than Barrault to make its poetry tangible to a newer audience. The moment has perhaps arrived to release all the symbolic power these texts conceal, rather than treat Camus, whether out of malice or respect, as a veteran in "committed" literature. Could the time be riper? After long participation in wars hot and cold, literature seems to have been honorably discharged. The pure practice of language is fashionable once more. Criticism now tends to concentrate its attention on the system of signs, forms, and images that writers invent to transmit messages in themselves alien to art. The time has come to return Camus to literature, to recognize the ambiguous quality in his books suggested by several of their titles: *The Wrong Side and the Right Side, Exile and the Kingdom*. Here is an opportunity to make reparation for the fate of Jonas,* trapped by his fame, who is destroyed by the pressure of his admirers.

Admiration is tyrannical; friendship, in contrast, is generous. The latter is what Camus needs in order to be seen as himself once more. Perhaps among his posthumous

---

* Protagonist in *The Artist at Work*, one of the six short stories that make up *Exile and the Kingdom*. [E.C.K.]

readers he will find the "true and fabled friends" of whom he complained, in the secrecy of his *Notebooks*, that he had been deprived: "Every last one of them is out to destroy me, relentlessly demanding their share, without ever, ever stretching out a hand to me, coming to my aid, loving me at last for what I am, so that I can remain what I am" (*Notebooks*, unpublished).

But who, then, is this misunderstood writer one is to love at last for his true self? In wishing for friendship that would help him "remain" what he was, Camus implicitly defined himself as a faithful being. His whole work, in fact, whether lyrical or rational, is a monument of fidelity. It repeats itself. It reveals obsessions, and not least among them—from *The Stranger* to *The Plague*, from *The Just Assassins* to *The Fall*—the obsession with trial and judgment. His work deepens, from *Death in the Soul* to *The Misunderstanding*, from *Nuptials at Tipasa* to *Return to Tipasa* (is this the influence of Nietzsche's myth of the eternal return?)—deepening rather than taking new shapes. It is unaware of betrayals, whose evil Camus seems to exorcise in recounting the demoniac adventure of a "renegade."* Taut to the point of rigidity in his wish for coherence, his work would be ill suited to metamorphoses and conversions. Camus, then, invents little. Out of impotence, or intentionally? He keeps a tight rein on such imagination, doubtless limited, as he has at his disposal. He loosens the reins rarely, as in the rhapsodic *The Sea Close By*. He forbids himself the role of prophet, of anticipating the future like Huxley or Breton, of yielding in his work to idle fancies of hope. The gifts of life at hand are more precious to him. But he celebrates them with measure. The poet of *Nuptials* is an ascetic, not a sybarite. The radical novelty

---

* *The Renegade*—another of the novellas that make up *Exile and the Kingdom*. [E.C.K.]

of each moment is not sufficient to arrest and nourish his musing. He is not the man to practice the virtue of *disponibilité* (invariable openness or availability) that Gide, one of his first masters, preached: "Happy he who is attached to nothing on earth and brings eternal fervor to what is constantly in motion" (André Gide, *Les Nourritures terrestres*, IV; *Romans . . . Oeuvres lyriques*, p. 184). Camus is not Nathanael's brother. To Gidian fervor, as well as to Christian hope, he prefers fidelity, or at least the "promise of fidelity that each true artist, every day, makes himself, in silence" (final words of Camus's Nobel Prize acceptance speech, *Essais*, p. 1075). The Kingdom he opposes to Exile belongs to the past. It is a Paradise lost. The awareness of *Summer in Algiers*—"It is a well-known fact that we always recognize our homeland at the moment we are about to lose it" (*Lyrical . . . Essays*, p. 90)—becomes in *The Myth of Sisyphus* the universal maxim: "Nostalgia . . . illustrates the essential impulse of the human drama" (p. 17).

To speak of nostalgia is to speak of homesickness. Camus is quite naturally tempted to follow the example of Ulysses. He is always longing to see his homeland once more. In 1936, well before he was subjected to the trial of exile, he had only to find himself wandering the streets of Prague—under the weight of a violent emotional shock, it is true—for the memory of those summer evenings of his adolescent years, "gentle summer evenings that I love so much, suffused in green light and filled with young and beautiful women" (*Lyrical . . . Essays*, pp. 46, 47), to obsess him and make him yearn for home. In *A Happy Death* this odyssey becomes a fictitious itinerary. Patrice Mersault—wanting to travel, the better to rejoice in his emancipation after murdering Zagreus—finds in his turn on the banks of the Vltava, despite the fascination of baroque art, "a solitude in which love had no part" (p. 68). He feels "a nostalgia for cities filled with sunlight and women, with the green evenings that close all wounds" (p. 71). There is nothing left for him, either, but to return to Algiers, to the "House Above the World" where his three friends, the "little grinds," await him. The fascination with primitive beaches is so strong that it enthralls the somber Martha of *The Misunderstanding*, who does not know them, but dreams about them. At last, in *Return to Tipasa*, the prodigal son comes home.

Yet Camus, who remembers having been a philosopher, only permits himself to be taken in just so far by the illusions of nostalgia. His nostalgia lies well below the sentimental surface of the self where the regrets of a Du Bellay reside. This exile does not imagine that his anguish will cease at the mere rediscovery of his homeland. He knows the vanity of pilgrimages. Retracing his own path at Tipasa step by step in 1953, he does not fail to confront the unavoidable warning: "It is certainly a great folly, and one that is almost always punished, to go back to the places of one's youth, to want to relive at forty the things one loved or greatly enjoyed at twenty" (*Lyrical . . . Essays*, p. 163). If he permits himself the folly of "hoving into home port" despite all this, it is in order to penetrate, as René Char does, a "lost truth"—more familiar to Plotinus than to geographers—that "each day now brings us closer to, although for a long time we were able only to say that it was our country, and that far from it we suffered, as if in exile" (Camus, on René Char, *Lyrical . . . Essays*, p. 325).

For once, absorbed in the promise received from a poet who was also his friend, Camus makes reference to a Kingdom in the future: "But words finally take shape, light dawns, one day the country will receive its name. Today a poet describes it for us, magnificently, reminding us, already, to justify the present, that this country is 'earth and murmurs, amid the impersonal stars'" (p. 325). But in other circumstances, restored to his own inspiration, Camus, like Proust, delves into his memory. He gives the name Kingdom to the land of his birth, confessing his homesickness for Algeria. How great was his anguish in 1958 when he realized that the holy land of his memories must alter! Death would spare him the unhappiness of losing once more and forever what recognizably had been truly his homeland. But enough of this pathetic tone. It betrays the fidelity that linked Camus to his "lost truth," which must not be confused—this is all too clear—with the usual feeling of nostalgia. Camus's is entirely of the spirit. Difficult to live with, it is difficult to express as well. For a long time Camus only let it be perceived through his fiction. But the moment finally came, with the republication of *The Wrong Side and the Right Side* (1958), when he would unveil its secrets. Rereading his first book, which dates from 1937, he was astounded to find in it the model not only of his later writings, but also of that totally truthful work he had not yet produced and perhaps never would produce. In his personal and professional life, he had not ceased to follow resolutely the teaching of Gide's *Fruits of the Earth:* "Become what you are." Here he was, attaining full awareness of his faithfulness at the age of forty-five: "I know this," he writes, "with sure and certain knowledge: a man's work is nothing but this slow trek to rediscover, through the detours of art, those two or three great and simple images in whose presence his heart first opened. This is why, perhaps, after working and producing for twenty years, I still live with the idea that my work has not even begun" (*Lyrical . . . Essays,* pp. 16–17).

Camus's words remind one of Péguy, observing, about the "deaf preparations" of his youth, that "twenty, thirty years of strenuous labor, a whole lifetime of work will not do, will not undo, what has been done, or what has been undone once and for all" (Charles Péguy, *L'Argent*, p. 7). Such, in a sense, is the destiny of the modern artist. He does not shape his work as the classical artist did, by selecting a model borrowed from tradition and copying it. He invents it. Or at least he believes he is inventing it. But if he knows himself, he realizes that he, too, obeys some law of imitation, which, although it may be quite internal, is no less real. What else, indeed, permits him the freedom he believes he enjoys if not producing over and over, from sketches to masterpieces, without ever giving it final form, his own first vision of the world and of existence? Aware of the guiding principle that governed his career, acknowledging it in the preface to *The Wrong Side and the Right Side*, Camus decides to assume full responsibility for it. He sets himself the task of devoting a whole novel to the model he has always followed, the Platonic idea* each of his successive books has only caught shadows of, dancing on the cavern wall. In his *Notebooks* during December, 1938, Camus wrote: "Death and a writer's work. Just before dying, he has his last work read over to him. He still hasn't said what he had to say. He orders it to be burned. And he dies with nothing to console him—and with something snapping in his heart like a broken chord" (*Notebooks 1935-1942*, p. 108). As if wishing to deny that tragic presentiment of his youth, Camus laid out his plan for *The First Man*.†

Who, then, is this "first man," first not only in time,

---

* In Platonic philosophy, a love transcending the feeling for the individual, rising to ecstasy in contemplation of universal patterns and the ideal. [E.C.K.]

† *The First Man* is the final novel Camus left unfinished at the time of his accidental death in 1960. At this writing, its fragments have not yet been published even in France. [E.C.K.]

whom it is still "after working and producing for twenty years" Camus's task to achieve and set at the heart of a fable, who resembles himself? At first the writer identifies this character with his own father. Thinking of himself, Camus writes: "What he had sought avidly to know through books and human beings seemed to him now a secret lost with this dead man, with what he had been and what had become of him, and that he, too, had sought very far for what was close at hand." Yet the tomb at Saint-Brieuc, where the soldier fallen at the Marne lies forever sleeping, remains an enigma. At Solferino, the little farm on the Saint-Apôtre estate where his son was born is now occupied by foreign settlers. And what's to be learned from the dead man's widow? Nothing, not even maternal love can free her from her silence. Camus, then, did not receive the underlying theme of his novels, his lyric prose, his plays as a legacy. It is he, the orphan from Belcourt, who is the "first man," the model he sketched so many times, whose portrait he wished to achieve. This first Camus, the "son of no one," remains to be discovered.

Chapter II

Dreaming

> Let's keep on dreaming, it doesn't
> cost a thing.
>
> —Jehan Rictus, *Poor Man's Soliloquies*

In Camus's literary experiments as a teen-ager, there is one word that frequently recurs, "lassitude."* The Nietzschean Fool, who has a dialogue with the narrator of *Back Again to Myself*, would like to conclude the interview with this paradox: "Seek in order not to find. Always. For you are much too tormented to abandon the quest. . . . But, you see, we shall at least have found something."—"What?" said I.—"Lassitude" (see p. 172). But his interlocutor is only half satisfied. Even though Gide had praised the attraction of "anticipations,"† Camus's person could not prefer the "hunt" to the "capture." He suffers from his "lassitude" and would rather admit it as does his music-lover in *Uncertainty*: "For myself, I am weary, horribly weary. Weary of searching for truth and happiness . . . weary of everything, incapable of seeking and of acting, feeding on my lassitude" (see p. 164). Yes, the young Camus, at the age of about twenty, was passing through a crisis of discouragement, ill concealed in a show of elegant nonchalance. The ordeal of an illness he was not cured of painfully exacerbated his love of life. He threw himself upon the "fruits of the earth." But without the taboos of a puritan education to vanquish, Camus had no

---

* A Nietzschean idea. Cf. *Ainsi parlait Zarathoustra*, III, 18. [P.V.]

† Gide, *Cahiers d'André Walter*: "Life is all in anticipation," p. 94. *Les Nourritures terrestres* 1, I: "May each anticipation within you be not even a desire, but simply a disposition for acceptance," p. 31. [P.V.]

victories to sing of. He was too aware of the bitterness that follows pleasure for Gidian hedonism to be enough to make him happy. Like a good Algerian, he recalls that the flesh he worships is perishable. He does not dissociate images of death from those of life (*Summer in Algiers, Lyrical . . . Essays*, p. 88). His fervor is already tragic.

But Camus is also weary of the poverty—Péguy would doubtless call it the destitution—in which he has lived with his family. About the humiliations poverty inflicted on him, he is proudly silent with the young bourgeois who have become his friends. But they still hurt. What bitterness there is in the disgust Zagreus reveals at the beginning of *A Happy Death!* ". . . We use up our lives making money, when we should be using our money to gain time. . . . To have money is to have time. . . . Time can be bought. Everything can be bought" (*A Happy Death*, p. 43). And what violence there is in Mersault's resolution to kill and rob his protector in order to assure himself the means of living free! Camus, in these early writings, keeps harking back to the cruel experience of his entry into the world of the well-provided-for. It will be a long time before he is relieved of certain secrets, projecting onto Jacques Cormery, hero of *The First Man*, for example, "the shame and the shame of being ashamed" that Camus himself had felt when, accepted at the Lycée Bugeaud, he was about to write "domestic" on his identity card, next to the heading "parent's occupation."

How can he forgive himself this wretched thought and many others, too? Perhaps only in the reassurance of being loved by God? But the young Camus despairs of receiving that kind of help. If he reads the Bible (see Max-Pol Fouchet's *Un jour, je m'en souviens*, p. 18), he does not accept it as Revelation. Of his first communion, hastily prepared and received before the competition for scholarships, Camus retains nothing but the memory "of a nameless mystery, with which the divine persons named and rigorously defined by the catechism had no connection whatever." Since that time, the religious information a quick-tempered priest had refused him is drawn from his readings. Camus studies the mystics, particularly Theresa of Avila. He meditates on Pascal and Saint Augustine. On the advice of his teacher Jean Grenier, he is also becoming interested in the sacred writings of India. He praises Claudel for having "understood" that "man is nothing by himself alone and that he must give himself to something higher." He could take heed himself of his Fool's avowal: "The truth is that I am trying to believe." When he drafts *Art in Communion,* he chooses as an epigraph the Pascalian formula: "And I can only approve of those who seek with lamentation." He gives proof of the same good will as do the libertines to whom Pascal's *Thoughts on Religion and Evidence of Christianity* was addressed. But Camus also and above all shares their confusion, if one continues to trust the testimony of *Art in Communion:* "When a young man finds himself at the threshold of life, on the brink of any undertaking, he often feels grave weariness and profound disgust at the pettiness and vanities that have soiled him even as he tried to deny them; an instinctive aversion rises in him. . . . He doubts: ideas in general, social conventions, everything he has received. A graver matter, he also doubts the deepest feelings: Faith, Love. He becomes aware that he is nothing. There he is, alone, and at a loss." Weary of doubting, the young freethinker seeks consolation in humor. One fine day, he imagines a God as alone, as naked, and as much in distress as himself, who speaks to his soul and complains of his destiny as an inaccessible God: "In the end, I'm bored. Because, in point of fact, for thousands of years I have been alone. And it is useless for writers to tell me solitude makes for grandeur; I am not a writer, myself. . . . The truth is I'm bored. Omniscience, omnipotence, it's always a bit the same thing" (*God's Dialogue with His Soul;* see p. 207).

But Camus is most often serious. He proposes to understand his "lassitude" rather than put if off on God. Philosophical reflection, into which Grenier initiates him, helps him diagnose his illness. He learns to analyze the "desire for unity, for the absolute," for "participation" that torments him and that is not the attribute, despite the sociologists, of the mentality called primitive (see Camus's dissertation, dated August, 1933, on "the logic of pre-logic"). He finds it again in Plotinus, and applies himself to following by means of thought the "hypostases" that lead the soul to the contemplation of the One. He admires that "meditation of the solitary person, in love with the world to the extent that it is only a crystal in which the divinity can act"; that "thinking filled with the silent rhythms of the stars, but uneasy about the God who commands them" (*Métaphysique chrétienne et néo-platonisme*, III, I, *d*(Pléiade), *Essais*, p. 1286). Yet, introduced to that handsome edifice, the *Enneads*, Camus notices perhaps that his mind, if he lends himself to theoretical speculation, sticks to systems with difficulty. From this stems the attraction that Bergson's intuitive philosophy has for him. Will it be the philosophy of the century, a culture that brings together mankind's irrational strengths? Doubtless he hopes so. But how disappointed he is when Henri Bergson publishes *The Two Sources of Morality and Religion*! Camus confesses this in one of his first published pieces, an article in the magazine *Sud* (June, 1932). He is going on nineteen: "People . . . anticipated a sort of scripture invented by the intuition, which should have been understood intuitively. . . . What greater destiny could Bergson have dreamed of for his philosophy? . . . *The Two Sources of Morality and Religion* disappointed me. . . . Bergson has not completed his work. . . . But perhaps another philosopher will come along, younger, more daring . . . Then, perhaps, we shall have the philosophy-religion, that gospel of the century, for want of which the contemporary mind grievously wanders" (see pp. 127, 128).

It is tempting to suppose that the young critic was aspiring to compensate for the waning master and invent that "philosophy-religion," that "gospel of the century." But it would be imprudent to discern too soon in Camus the future moralist of *The Myth of Sisyphus* and *The Rebel*. "I am not a philosopher," he would answer in 1945 in an interview with the periodical *Servir* (see *Essais*, p. 1427). His early writings attest to the sincerity of this statement. It is on art, actually, rather than on philosophy that Grenier's student relies to reduce his "lassitude." He sees in it a happy evasion that, at will, procures the oblivion of dreams. The remedy fits the illness. Can one conceive of the want, both material and moral, in which Camus spent his childhood, surrounded by people who were exemplary but poorly educated and almost mute? For him there was no refuge more natural than oblivion and no oblivion more innocent than dreaming, the better to keep him from some guilty lack of loyalty. Very young, then, he dreams, and dreams a great deal. But he dreams still better as he learns to read. For this son of illiterates, the unreal world of books is a doubly guarded Paradise. The elementary school textbooks, conceived for children of metropolitan France, threw open the doors to an extraordinary world. In them he encounters "children with woolen hats and scarves, their feet in wooden clogs, who make their way home in the icy cold, trailing their shoes across snow-covered roads, until they make out the snowy rooftop of their house, where chimney smoke signals that pea soup is cooking on the hearth." Camus, in turn, depicts these features in his compositions. He becomes so used to escaping from reality into fiction that when M. Germain, the teacher, reads *The Wooden Crosses* aloud, a parallel between Dorgelès's story and his own father's fate of having "died for France" never occurs to him. Rather, Camus is fascinated to make the acquaintance of legendary heroes "clothed in heavy materials stiffened by the mud, who speak a strange language and live in ditches under the barrage of shellfire, rockets, and bullets." The glorious entertainment continues at home, beneath the gas lamp and despite unwelcome protests from his grandmother. The schoolboy devours volumes of *The Intrepid Ones*, the *Pardaillans*, and then *The Three Musketeers*. As he grows older, he organizes his passion better. Every Thursday, he is off to the city library. At the very entrance, he inhales the sacred odor of bindings, takes in the shelves filled with dreams, waits for the inspiration that will settle his choice, religiously lending himself to the rites of borrowing. In the street, he hurriedly leafs through the books he is carrying to find the first fruits of his weekly feast. Joyously he rediscovers that innocent universe in which wealth and poverty are equally interesting because they are "perfectly unreal." And with tender respect Camus's mother would stroke the head of her prodigal son. He was enjoying access to a life she had never known.

At the same age, Sartre had a quite different experience of reading. Far from separating him from his family, who were of the cultivated bourgeoisie, reading gave him fuller membership in their community. Reading was part of his education. A whole career of writing and, above all, a serious examination of work achieved would be needed to teach him he had fallen into the trap of words and that reality remained inaccessible to him. The divorce between literature and living that Sartre became aware of very late, Camus on the other hand discovered even as he was learning how to read. And his situation as a poor child made him cherish it from the first. If he appreciated the *Poor Man's Soliloquies*, it was not because Jehan Rictus sacrificed a certain realism, but because he sang of his hero's dreams:

Let's keep on dreaming, it doesn't cost a thing.*

All the arts, in fact, find their justification in a common rejection of reality. Camus, dazzled by Schopenhauer's and Nietzsche's aesthetics, and guided by comrades who had had the opportunity of a musical education, convinced himself that Beethoven, Chopin, and Wagner could cure him of his "lassitude." In his *Essay on Music*— a text more ambitious, it is true, than profound—which Camus sent to the magazine *Sud* in June, 1932, he complacently develops this conviction. He defines music as "the expression of an ideal world" and he dreams of the promise of "redemption," which, according to him, it contains: "With the possibility of living in a purer world, free of pettiness . . . man will forget his vulgar wants and his ignoble appetites. He will live intensely that life of the spirit which must be the goal of all existence. . . . Musset was very true and very profound when he said jokingly: 'It's Music that made me believe in God.' "†
With *Art in Communion,* the intrepid dreamer completes his theory. Here he analyzes the architecture of the Arab house, with the intention of demonstrating that its special effect comes from a sudden and startling escape to the privacy of the patio, after a dome-like entrance and long corridor. "One can make this architectural device," he

* Quoted in Camus's article, in the magazine *Sud* (May, 1932), *Jehan Rictus, the Poet of Poverty.* [P.V.] See p. 120. [E.C.K.]

† This does not figure in the extracts of the *Essay on Music* in the Pléiade edition of Camus's *Essais*, pp. 1200–1203. [P.V.]

specifies, "correspond to a sort of affective principle; if one thinks of the restlessness that floats beneath the dome of the entryway, plunging into the uncertain attraction of the blue corridor, illuminated a first time only to rediscover a winding corridor before it arrives at the infinite truth of the patio, can one not believe that from dome to patio a desire for evasion is developed that responds exactly to the Oriental soul?" One does not know if Camus's architect friend Jean de Maisonseul knew about this page, nor if he agreed with his friend. This first aesthetic theory that Camus professed seems more solid when he verifies its principles by contemplating the frescoes of Giotto, in which, defying the laws of movement, the "characters are fixed in the silence of a perfect action" and their silhouettes overwhelm the background in such a way as to "restore man to his spiritual preeminence." But of course it is the unreality of literature that this senior at the lycée of Algiers prefers to discuss. The good M. Mathieu cannot get his student to establish nuances in his thesis so that it respects the data of literary history. There is nothing he can do but fault a new plagiarism of Nietszche when he discovers this peremptory conclusion in a dissertation on the relationship of tragedy and comedy: "Greek tragedy is born of the need to flee from a too painful life. Not seeking to make life more agreeable, the Greeks annihilated it by means of tragedy, by means of the dream. What Schiller called 'Greek naiveté' was only the faculty of making life disappear and of dreaming. This seductive and disturbing hypothesis seems to us particularly fitting in the case under examination. Tragedy, like comedy, would have no other goal but to bring forgetfulness" (Camus, dissertation on "tragedy and comedy," 1932).

To dream, to dream with pen in hand, in order to forget his "lassitude," this is what Camus is attempting in many of his early essays. Under the Bergsonian title *Intuitions*, in October, 1932, he puts together a series of texts, which he himself presents as "reveries": "These reveries were born of great lassitude. They record the desire of a too mystical soul, in search of an object for its fervor and its faith. If they are sometimes despondent, it is because there was no one to accept their ardor. If they are sometimes negative, it is because no one wanted their affirmations. But despite the errors, the hesitations, the tedium, and the lassitude, the fervor remains, ready for superhuman communions and impossible actions." *Intuitions* puts characters onstage who are not engaged in any action: a young man, an old man, a melomaniac, a fool.* They are very much "loonies" (*des mangeurs de lune*), one and all, brothers of Baudelaire's "stranger," in love with the "marvelous clouds," which Camus and his friend Fréminville cross-examine aloud, in two voices, as they stroll along the streets of Algiers (Jeanne Delais, *L'Ami de chaque matin*, p. 117). Yet they enclose themselves in a common room. Rather than leaving them to their respective chimeras, Camus manages a dialogue between the two that permits him to express his own thoughts. One divines that he is recalling *Thus Spake Zarathustra*. But Nietzsche's lyricism and imagination are lacking. Camus seems more apt at imitations of Gide's treatises.† He is, despite himself, resisting the temptation to daydream, doubtless less congenial to his still unformed talent than he would like. Inconvenient, too, to someone of his shy character.

Will Camus abandon his plans to escape into literature as a result of this failure? The love of a young girl inspires him with the desire to make one more attempt, which will be the last. Simone Hié, whom he marries June 16, 1934, is an avid reader of fairy tales. He sees her

---

* Fool in the sense of madman, rather than jester. [E.C.K.]

† Reference to *Narcissus* and other early writings of Gide. [E.C.K.]

through Merlin's eyes. He cherishes in her another Melusina. She loosens the knots of his too rigid sensibility. He wanted to fantasize in his writings but did not dare to. She gives him this audacity. It is spontaneously his, one morning before leaving the house, when he writes the tender note that will greet his sleeping beauty when she wakens: "We would like to break the too narrow limits of thought and of humanity, beyond Time, beyond Space. And since we wish it, it is as good as done. I shall take my little one by the hand and seat her next to me. There, she will gaze at me for a long time, and in one another's eyes we will follow the slow navigations toward the unknown seas that Sinbad's vessel charted. Look, here we are." But there is something still better to come. On the first Christmas of their life together, Camus leaves on a table or slips into his partner's slipper (perhaps a fur slipper?) *Melusina's Book*—a thin school notebook containing a fairy tale and the account of two dreams, one experienced by a fairy, the other by a child.

In the prologue to the *Tale for Some Too Sad Children*, Camus announces his intention to flee from banal life to the realm of enchanted creatures. "It is time to speak of the fairies. In order to escape from the intrepid melancholy of expectation, it is time to create new worlds. Do not believe, though, that fairy tales lie. He who tells them lies—but as soon as it is told, the fairy miracle slowly floats up into the air and goes off to live its life, real, truer than the insolence of everyday." The hoped-for miracle is produced more than once. A certain gaiety animates *Melusina's Book*. Gone is much of the clumsiness that hampered the movement of his *Intuitions*. The characters seek to live. The good will of the fairy who dances and sings contrasts prettily with the rigidity of the proud cavalier who rides, palfrey pointed straight ahead, without lowering his lance or turning his eyes. The discretion of the cat who silently ambles toward the woods, completely caught up in anticipation of the happiness that awaits him, evokes the reader's sympathy.

But with *The Fairy's Dream* and *The Boats* the tone changes. From being playful it becomes grave. The fairy throws herself into a dream that becomes deranged. As the child makes his way at night under cover through the forest, he gives way to uncontrolled emotions. In both cases the story, scarcely begun, stops short. An irrepressible lyricism invades and interrupts it. Aware of this failing, Camus attempts to cover it up. He pretends to be accomplishing some secret goal. "Thus have I often wished," he pretends, "for a tale that was only a beginning and left hanging, deliciously unfinished." A phony confession. Actually, the apprentice storyteller feels ill at ease. Why are there, even in the first and most successful of the three little pieces in *Melusina's Book*, so many meanderings? Why, for example, all those questions as he is about to name the fitting animal to bring the fairy and the knight together? "What will this animal be? A bird? Birds have the nasty habit of disturbing the poetry of landscapes with their songs. A dog? Too hackneyed. Better a cat, taking care to remove his boots so as to avoid being commonplace." Camus seems to force his talent. In vain does he parade his hesitations, underline his asides, make fun of himself; the "great inventive qualities" he would need to persevere are lacking. His imagination lends itself to the play of a certain kind of fantasy, but he has no feel for fairy tales. Nor can he long sustain the impulse of gratuitous reverie. Unaware of his true vocation, he does not yet think of condemning "games of intellectual iridescence," as he will later on in an article on Giraudoux's *Ondine* (*Jean Giraudoux, ou Byzance au théâtre*, from *La Lumière*, May 10, 1940; *Essais*, pp. 1404–1409). But he retreats from them spontaneously. Other, more serious experiments call out to him. In presenting his cat, he does not fail to challenge the superiority that man claims over animal; the tale nearly becomes a fable and might defend La Fontaine's moral in his *Discourse to Madame de la Sablière*.* But, usually, it is the author's asides to the reader that reduce these flights of fancy. "What good would a fairy be," Camus wonders, "if there were nothing human about her?" His enchanted creature, "who lives for her moment and laughs with her flowers," who loves music and dancing, resembles the young woman for whom *Melusina's Book* was written. The austere knight who moves forward on "a great pretentious road" toward the "sky," instead of disporting himself "on the little garden path" leading to the sleeping beauty, is the storyteller's double. But the cat, who is better endowed for the pursuit of happiness, could also be his double. Camus recognizes himself so well in each of these two characters, he is so little absent from his story, that he ends up examining his own conscience: "Fairy tales, children's silences, oh! my realities, the only true, the only great ones, I should like to forget myself. Melusina, Morgana, Urgela, Vivian, fairies all, I am thirsty for your humanity. For I, too, wait, I seek, I hope, and do not want to find anything. Having no truth, I do not like great highways. But I like dry roads, sprinkled with hope. The dust of roads, the roughness of ditches are so much rapture for one who knows how to wait. Happiness from suffering, pride of constraint, oh! my realities, children's silences, fairy tales."

Beyond the personal "realities," Camus the storyteller hopes to achieve the essential reality of things and beings. *The Fairy's Dream* unveils "the world's 'beautiful secret.' " It opens eyes that do not know how to see upon "a too

---

* See Marianne Moore's translation, *To Tris: Madame de la Sablière, The Fables of La Fontaine* (New York: Viking, 1954), pp. 229–233. [E.C.K.]

beautiful world, unknown because ill seen," and "above all ill loved." He makes this world "spring forth" before us in full light, with the aid of love and music, which sharpen the senses. The experience of contemplation, the "reverie" that Camus exalts here beneath the guise of a whimsical tale are wholly the theme in *The Boats.* From this point on, fiction is nearly abandoned. No more fairy, no more cat, no more knight; only a nameless, faceless child, who might also be a poet, an adult capable of being astonished. Camus quite naturally identifies with him. The child is present, in person, in the middle of the clearing, near a pool where trickling water murmurs. It is he who notices and receives the forest's nocturnal song, who lives in "communion" with nature, who expects from love "the joy of tables filled with flowers, tables underneath the bowers." When at last, "toward evening, on the trembling water, a timely but surprising flight of boats scatters and slowly moves away toward the horizon," the child from the "poor quarter" abandons himself to quasi-Proustian reminiscence, resurrecting a memory that is his alone, destined to appear again on a page of *The Wrong Side and the Right Side.*

Melusina's Book departs appreciably from the attempt at imaginary flight set forth in the *Tale for Some Too Sad Children.* Camus does not accomplish the great leap into a dream world that inspired Baudelaire's *Invitation to the Voyage* or Fauré's melodies in *L'Horizon chimérique.* Was his luck any better a year earlier, when he wrote *Bériha or the Dreamer?* The text has disappeared. But it seems unlikely this attempt was any more successful than *Melusina's Book.* In a letter to Max-Pol Fouchet, Camus defends himself rather badly against his friend's reproach that he had sacrificed dreaming for "logic." Short on proofs, Camus makes peremptory affirmations: "Bériha is the dreamer. The Dream is reality disordered. I set both Dream and Action above logic" (*Essais,* p. 1206).

Dreaming

Such confidence is surprising from a man prey to dreams, or, as Breton would say, from a "definitive dreamer." Camus will not be another Nerval. After *Bériha*, it is *Melusina's Book* that he leaves unfinished. He remains a Sunday storyteller.

Chapter III

Bearing Witness

Stop transferring poetry into dream;
know how to see it in reality.

—Gide, *New Fruits of the Earth*

The semi-failure of *Bériha* and *Melusina's Book* is not,
however, as serious as one might fear. It is no prejudg-
ment of the future. In attempting to write these tales,
Camus had already—not much earlier, it is true, but very
consciously—rejected his initial idea of what literature
consisted of, when in his "lassitude" he dreamed only of
"escape." What caused this turnabout was the reading
of a book, André de Richaud's *La Douleur* (*Pain*), which
Jean Grenier lent Camus in 1931, during his second year
of philosophy. The teen-ager transferred to *La Douleur*
the admiration he had reserved until then for *Fruits of the
Earth*. He was probably drawn to Richaud because the
jury for a literary prize had been so unjust as to deny
recognition to the superiority of this beautiful tale about
the love of a German prisoner of war and the widow of
a French officer, whose utterly pagan lyricism "streams
with innocence."* But a much deeper motive determined
his attitude. For the first time, a book reflected the image
and revealed to him secrets of his own existence. In
Thérèse Delombre he met a second mother, beautiful,
tender, and condemned to solitude. When she falls in
love with Otto Rulf, Camus immediately divines what
the visits of M. Antoine, the Maltese fish merchant, used
to mean to his own mother, Catherine Camus, until his

* From the book jacket of André de Richaud's *La Douleur*,
quoted from an article by Le Grix (November, 1930). [P.V.]

Uncle Ernest threw the unfortunate suitor down the stairs. Camus recognized himself in little George. Perhaps, without admitting it, he, too, had felt the jealousy that the orphan in Richaud's novel focuses on Otto. What does it matter if the episodes in the novel do not always recreate the scenes of his own childhood. They exude the same air Camus had breathed: "The child grew up in an atmosphere of sadness and love"; the same "anguish" prevailed in both, one of fierce and secret passion. Richaud's world, finally, was very much Camus's own childhood world, reduced to the plainness of naked sensation, its "paths overgrown by a thousand plants in full blossom," and all the fragrances that "rise from the earth."

Camus did not immediately pick out these affinities. The existence of a book that opened up to him not dreams but life left him dumfounded and in awe. Thirty years later, he could still recall the miracle, but had become capable of explaining it to himself: "I have never forgotten his admirable book, the first to speak to me of what I knew: a mother, poverty, fine evening skies. It loosened a tangle of obscure bonds within me, freed me from fetters whose hindrance I felt without being able to give them a name. I read it in one night, in the best tradition, and the next morning, armed with a strange new liberty, went hesitatingly forward into unknown territory. I had just learned that books dispensed things other than forgetfulness and entertainment. My obstinate silences, this vague but all-pervasive suffering, the strange world that surrounded me, the nobility of my family, their poverty, my secrets, all this, I realized, could be expressed! There was a deliverance, an order of truth, in which poverty, for example, suddenly took on its true face, the one I had suspected it possessed, that I somehow revered."* Among Camus's rare confidences,

* *Lyrical . . . Essays*, p. 249. [P.V.]

there are few as precious as this one, permitting one to
pinpoint the moment he perceived that literature offered
him a "deliverance" much preferable to the "oblivion"
of dreams: the comfort of the truth expressed in words,
of "suffering" called by its name.

*Sois sage, ô ma douleur, et tiens-toi plus tranquille.**

It also puts the emphasis on the "discomfort" Camus
hoped to vanquish by following Richaud's example. What
was it, then, that made him suffer, before he devoured
La Douleur "in one night," if not secrets within that were
stifling him? And of what are such secrets made if not,
above all, like all secrets, of the silence that keeps them?
Any writer worthy of the name raises his voice in order
to break, without betraying it, a certain silence. "Silence,"
said Vigny, "is Poetry itself to me." Camus's work, more
than any other, is born of silence. As far as he could
reach back into his memories, indeed, he would run up
against the absence or the impotence of language. He was
unable to recall anything his father said. He was raised
by a mother condemned to be mute by who knows what
inhibition of the voice. He suffered from the inadequacy
of her conversation. He evokes her sadly in one of the
stories in *Voices from the Poor Quarter* omitted from
The Wrong Side and the Right Side, no doubt, out of his
sense of discretion. "He had had a mother. Sometimes she
would be asked a question: 'What are you thinking about?
—'Nothing,' she would answer.—And it was very true.
. . . Her life, her interests, her children were simply
there, with a presence too natural to be felt. . . . Yet one

---

* From Baudelaire's poem *Recueillement*. [P.V.] "Be wise, oh my
pain, and give yourself more ease." In Robert Lowell's translation,
this poem is titled *Meditation*, and the line here quoted reads:
"Calm down, my sorrow, we must move with care." [E.C.K.]

of the children suffers over these attitudes. . . . He feels sorry for his mother; is this the same as loving her? She has never hugged or kissed him, for she wouldn't know how. . . . In a few moments, the old woman will return, life will start up again. . . . Meanwhile, the silence marks a pause, a moment of eternity. . . . The child will grow, will learn. . . . His mother will always have these silences. And always the child will question himself as well as his mother. . . . His grandmother will die, then his mother, then he. And, beside the cold stones, there will be neither question nor answer, a final silence."*

The "silences of childhood" evoked in the *Tale for Some Too Sad Children* take on their full meaning here. Never was a plural more expressive. There are the mother's silences, but also those of the mute uncle, of the grandmother who only resorts to speech in order to give orders and dispense scoldings. There are the silences of a child who cannot confide in anyone, since no one listens, who encloses himself in a world of books inaccessible to his family and who, when he becomes a student at the lycée, is neither able nor willing to express these experiences of solitude to his garrulous classmates. Camus had learned to speak, not to express himself. He lived in a silence he thought was "final," like that of the tomb. Language, which he manipulated skillfully enough to compose papers with which his teachers were satisfied, had not become an instrument of communication for him. The mute woman's son was keeping his secrets. He was not counting on the keenness of words to cut the "tangle of obscure bonds" that held him by the throat.

"When someone speaks, day breaks." Freud's ringing phrase is suddenly confirmed. In speaking out about himself, Richaud offers Camus the chance of beginning

---

* With a very few changes, this passage appears on pp. 32–34 of *Between Yes and No* in *Lyrical . . . Essays.* [E.C.K.]

a healthy relationship with language. He brings light
into the darkness of those "obstinate silences." He con-
vinces Camus that all can "be expressed"—above all, those
things the most taciturn being has lived through, seen,
or felt. After the revelation and the practical example of a
literature that is handmaiden of the truth will come, it is
true, the fear of being "misunderstood." Camus will ask
then, along with Brice Parain, "whether or not our language is false at the very moment when we think we are
telling the truth" (*Lyrical . . . Essays*, p. 229–230),
whether it "does not, in short, express man's final solitude
in a silent universe" (p. 230). He will agree that one
ought to believe in the God who has given men proof of
his paternity by addressing to them words to utterly remove such doubt. But in his "passionate unbelief," he
will keep the conviction that "man's great task is not to
serve the falsehood" (p. 238). He will confess it with
more modesty, but not with less ardor than at the moment
he acquires it by reading *La Douleur:* "The miracle consists of going back to everyday words, bringing to them
the honesty needed to lessen the part of falsehood and
hatred" (p. 239). Camus would continue to write and
make use of language, yearning "for the masterword that
would illuminate everything, for . . . this equivalent of
'*Aum*,' the sacred syllable of the Hindus" (p. 232).*

In 1931, the time of "homesickness" had not yet sur-
faced. Camus welcomes unreservedly the good tidings
Richaud has brought him. They are confirmed by several
of his mentors. Among those he most respects is Nietzsche,
who explains how the satirical chorus in Greek tragedy,
in comparison with the usual inventions of the art called
"civilized," "constitutes a truer, more real, and more

---

* Quotations are from Camus's book review of *On a Philosophy
of Expression*, by Brice Parain, in *Lyrical . . . Essays*, pp. 228–
241. [P.V.]

complete expression of existence" (Nietzsche, *La Naissance de la tragédie*, 8, p. 54). More broadly, he teaches Camus that "the realm of poetry does not reside outside the world like an imaginary figment born in a poet's mind," but that "it intends to be exactly the opposite, an unvarnished expression of the truth" (p. 54). Above all, Nietzsche proposed to him, in *Thus Spake Zarathustra*, the example of a chant, which, disdaining the false grace of rhetoric, the formalism of "scholars," and the academism of "consumptive souls," lays bare "the innocence of desire." Zarathustra laughs at "all lassitude," because he counts on the liberating force of language. Have not "names and sounds been given to men so that they may take pleasure in things?"* A whole literature Camus is well acquainted with derives from this Nietzschean aesthetic. For him, as for many of his contemporaries, *Fruits of the Earth* contains the promise of a literature that would make fun of literature in order to take the immediate experience of life more seriously. They recall the remark Gide slipped into his preface to the 1927 edition: "I wrote this book at a moment when literature reeked of the factitious and the confined, when it seemed to me urgent to make it touch the ground once more and simply set a bare foot upon the earth."† How pleased they would be when the master attempted, in *New Fruits of the Earth*, to go still further in the direction of simplicity: "I dream of new harmonies. An art of words, subtler and franker without rhetoric, that seeks to prove nothing" (*Les Nouvelles Nourritures*, I, 1; *Romans . . .* p. 257). One reads, too, in *The Immoralist:* "I aspire to nothing but the natural" (*Romans*, p. 431). Camus, in his turn, does not admire Gide blindly. He discerns the artifice that spoils the lyricism of the *Fruits* and observes

* *Ainsi parlait Zarathoustra*, p. 429. [P.V.]

† *Les Nourritures terrestres, Romans . . .* p. 249. [P.V.]

that "this vindication of the senses . . . is never anything but an intellectualization of the senses" (*Reading Notes*, April, 1933). He asks only to rediscover his first enthusiasm. Reading *The Counterfeiters*, Camus appreciates the honesty of "a writer struggling with Reality, which is opposed to what he wishes to make of it" (*Notes*, April, 1933). He does not deny Gide the merit of a necessary reaction against symbolist taste, whose preciosity the tragedy of the First World War had rendered insupportable once and for all.

It was precisely to the sons of those soldiers drafted into the First World War that Henry de Montherlant dedicated his work. Camus reacted to this appeal, which included him. "Montherlant struck me deeply then. *Unnecessary Service* is a book that moved me; not just by the elevation of its style" (Gabriel d'Aubarède, *Rencontre avec Albert Camus, Essais*, p. 1339). Camus no doubt welcomed sympathetically the sometimes untimely attacks that the author of *At the Fountains of Desire* launched against writers accused of dilettantism; against Barrès, for example: "a voyeur in war, a voyeur in religion" (Montherlant, *Aux fontaines du désir, Barrès s'éloigne, Essais*, p. 278). Even against Balzac and Flaubert: "Noble figureheads, glued to your [writing] tables, you have missed out on life" (*Aux fontaines, Palais Ben Ayed, Essais*, p. 317). In his so-called "enthrallments," Montherlant does not seek an evasion into the world of dreams, but "the realization, the putting into practice of its poetry, all the exquisite quality of things and beings with voluptuousness at their base" (Montherlant, *Essais*, p. 232). He relies upon his style, direct, abrupt, aggressive, to render without bombast that "lyrical state of mind" into which the simple presence of the world plunges him. This is how he transmits to Camus the dream of literary transparency that has perpetuated the heritage of Rousseau throughout the whole of modern literature.

André Malraux is not resigned to the status of "book-producer"* any more than Jean-Jaques Rousseau or Montherlant, nor to an imprisonment in his own words, like the "theoretical man-in-his-library" that Nietzsche mockingly portrays. Malraux's whole work is a testimony. If, in *The Temptation of the West*, he is uneasy about the future of European culture, it is with the feeling that he personally must answer for it; it is also because, living among them, he discovered the wisdom of the Orientals. Before *Man's Hope*, Malraux's novels *The Conquerors*, *The Royal Way*, and *Man's Fate* were born of his own experience with revolutionary adventure. He transposed this experience into the novelistic realm, taking care to avoid the affectations that often weaken the sincerity of confessions or personal anecdotes. The intensity, the violence of such experience are rendered with the vividness of a reporter's style. Malraux prefers the "instantaneous," which modern taste owes to the technique of photography, to the scene, to the tableau, to analysis. One guesses from this what Camus owes Malraux. He is indebted to Malraux—much more than he is to Gide, who remains a "belle-lettrist"—for the desire not to be dupe of empty words, the need for a certain literary asceticism. Malraux's example sustains Camus after reading *La Douleur*, when he begins his apprenticeship as a writer. Like a young painter who copies a famous canvas in order to strengthen his talent, Camus will follow Malraux by adapting Malraux's *The Time of Scorn†* to the stage. So much for a deliberate

---

* The word is Rousseau's: "I have made books, it's true, but I was never a 'book-producer.' " *Autres textes autobiographiques* (Pléiade), p. 840. [P.V.]

† Camus's adaptation was the first play staged by the Théâtre de l'Équipe. About its production at the Padovani Baths, consult the valuable record by Charles Poncet, quoted by Roger Quilliot, Camus's *Théâtre*, pp. 1688–1689. [P.V.]

imitation; but how many apparently original initiatives nonetheless carry the stamp of this master! Camus assimilates Malraux's inspiration so well that he bears witness to the revolutionary vocation of the Spanish people before Malraux does, by refusing to sign his own name as author of the play *Revolt in the Asturias* and by reducing the role of literature as much as possible in this anti-theatrical dramatic attempt: "Plays are not to be written, except as a last resort" (presentation note to *La Révolte dans les Asturies, Théâtre*, p. 399). Faithful to the very end to the lesson he has learned, Camus will impose the harsh discipline of journalism, the obligation to write under the pressure of the event itself. In writing *The Stranger*, he will no longer be anything but a chronicler.

While he is seeking his way, Camus has the good fortune to become the friend of a writer who, without having either the authority of Gide, Montherlant, or Malraux, or the charm of Richaud, is no less preoccupied, gently, subtly, and patiently, with making literature respectful of life. That writer is Jean Grenier. "I believe I already wanted to write at the time I discovered *Les Îles*," Camus would later say. "But I really decided to do so only after reading this book. . . . Even today, I find myself repeating, as if they were my own, phrases from *Les Îles* or other books by the same author" (*On Jean Grenier's "Les Îles," Lyrical . . . Essays*, p. 329). In fact, the immediate model for *The Wrong Side and the Right Side* is really this collection of purposely tame confessions. Grenier teaches Camus that for an artist worthy of the name there are no small subjects, but that the most modest subjects, as long as one has found them in one's own world, are satisfactory. Mouloud, the cat, merits a place in the bestiary of *Les Îles*, because he is seated before his master: "You may wonder how one can be interested in a cat, if the subject is worthy of a reasonable and thinking man who has ideas. . . . Ideas, good God! And yet the cat exists, and this is the difference that there is between him and those ideas" (Grenier, *Les Îles*, p. 32). The lesson Camus receives from Grenier is like the one Goethe gave Eckermann. The texts containing it "emanate from reality . . . finding in reality their foundation and their support." They respect, while expressing it, the silence with which the emotional life is surrounded when it becomes intensified. The whole poetic art of *Les Îles* consists of celebrating this silence, which every passionate teen-ager knows well: "At the moment when the tumult of a passion reaches its paroxysm," one reads in the passage devoted to the *Happy Isles*, "at this very moment there is a great silence in the soul. To take a familiar example, the silence of Julien Sorel in his prison. There is also the silence of the pilgrims of Emmaus;* the silence of the great morning of the Pentecost. Only Rembrandt, as far as I can see, knew how to express it completely. One can really sense that one second after this instant life will go on again, but that momentarily it is suspended by something that reaches infinitely beyond it" (p. 61). Without pretending to match Rembrandt in the representation of the mute scenes of the New Testament, Grenier does his best to emulate him in evoking certain introspective hours he experienced in Camus's land. The account of Grenier's walks among the rocks at Santa Cruz near Oran, the ruins of Tipasa, or the sands at Biskra record the same aesthetic. It is the model for the recitative in *Nuptials*.

Yet Camus does not show overnight that he can do as well as Grenier and the other writers from whom he has gained his new conception of literature. He takes time to meditate on the revelation he has received, which he

---

* The place outside Jerusalem where two of his disciples met the risen Christ. [E.C.K.]

means to draw upon for inspiration in his efforts. It is thus that he composes, in 1933, the profession of faith he calls *Art in Communion*. The temptation to flee from life into the world of art continues to work upon him. He gives way to it one more time. But he is quick to recover. Has he been reading Freud? One might think so to read his very lucid condemnation of what had been and remained his first impulse. "In Art, always struck by the ugliness of Reality," he observes, the adolescent "falls back on dreaming. But therein, alas! he rediscovers another reality with its beauty and its ugliness. Doubtless this is because through us Dream clings too closely to life. Despite what we do, and by our very existence, we unite these two apparent enemies. And the same disappointments await us in both." If dreams imitate "reality" (interior) to the point of reflecting its contradictions at least as obediently as the waking consciousness, they bring no liberation. Oblivion is impossible. Far better to make the best of the living world, beautiful or ugly, and control it by reproducing it in a work that will be faithful to it. The teen-ager Camus has taken as his spokesman ends up then by admitting that "Art" does not exist only in Dream. And he orients his literary projects in another direction. "He persuades himself that he must choose the object for Art from the flow of life and raise it above Space and Time. He understands that Art lies in the Pause, in Communion."

So much for large words and cumbersome capital letters! Camus is still a clumsy stylist, and the philosophy he is studying is going to his head. Yet, for all his lack of style, he has an intuitive sense that is not illusory. He has an idea that literature can detach an object from space or a moment from time so as to include them in a convenient fable. This is the miracle Vigny achieved with poetry, making use of it as a "preservative crystal." The miracle is produced again when Proust, his carriage stopping between the two church steeples in Martinville, repeats to himself and scribbles down the words that will immortalize the memory of his ride. "Without admitting to myself," he recalls, "that what lay buried within the steeples of Martinville must be something analagous to a charming phrase, since it was in the form of words that gave me pleasure that it had appeared to me, I borrowed a pencil and some paper . . . and composed, in spite of the jolting of the carriage, to appease my conscience and to satisfy my enthusiasm, the following little fragment, which I have since rediscovered and now reproduce, with only a slight revision here and there" (Proust, *Swann's Way*, tr. C. K. Scott Moncrieff [Vintage], p. 159). The budding aesthete of *Art in Communion* prays for a similar grace, giving it the name "Pause." Describing it in his own quite theoretical manner, he writes: "It seems, then, that all plenitude and all grandeur lie in the Pause. The plenitude of a gesture, of a work of art, is only realized if the former and the latter fix, by a limitation, some aspect of the fleeting nature of things in which we take delight. For the dreamy and sterile insignificance of evenings, one must substitute the work of art's more certain light." This poetic art leaves the most important role to the will, exaggerating perhaps the "constraint" that the work imposes on its model in "fixing" [or "immobilizing"] it. But it also calls for a submission to what is real, a receptivity, a generous impulse; in short, a "Communion" between the writer and that "aspect of the fleeting nature of things" that he has chosen to record. It is not, in fact, as in philosophical reflection, a matter of seeking "what lies beneath the delicate world of gesture and form. One must give oneself to it and communicate with it. We are weary of vain quests for the truth: nothing else can come of them but an offensive feeling of uselessness. The peculiar quality of Art is to 'fix into eternal formulas what flows in the uncertainty of appearances.' "

Camus thus quotes Schopenhauer, or paraphrases him. But now and then he achieves a more personal language. This is why the term "témoignage" ["giving testimony" or "bearing witness"] best translates the idea of literature he is developing for himself. He sticks to it in the letter he writes to Max-Pol Fouchet in 1934, while his friend is being cared for in France at the sanatorium in Saint-Hilaire-du-Touvet: "The only interest our little selves have," he writes, "is in the testimony we are able to offer about life. One offers it and goes one's way: that is what is called simplicity, and as the owner of the hotel in Tipasa says: 'a person could die without causing any talk' " (Fouchet, *Un jour, je m'en souviens*, p. 35). Gide, for his part, wrote in the *Cahiers d'André Walter:* "We live in order to make known, not in order to live" (*Essais*, p. 131). Camus is resolved to speak about himself before confronting the silence of death. He has no doubt that in so doing he risks becoming "a monstrous and talkative man." (This is how he will define himself in *The First Man.*) Nor does he suspect the ambiguity that is inherent in any testimony. Little by little, this will become apparent to him in its tragic dimension. Meanwhile, he devotes himself unreservedly to the literary vocation he has just discovered, and defines in his *Notebooks* in May, 1935: "The work of art is a confession, I must bear witness" (*Notebooks*, I, 4).

Chapter IV

Poverty

We Barbarians . . .

—Michelet, *Le Peuple*, preface
(letter to Edgar Quinet)

"Simplicity" demands that Camus give himself the means to write a chronicle of poverty. There is no experience more personal for him, when he chooses literature, than that of an almost complete destitution, aggravated by the infirmity of a silent mother. He was born poor and he remembers it. This is why, when one of his friends, Robert Pfister, founds the magazine *Sud*, Camus suggests an article on Jehan Rictus. It was the second in chronological order of two texts he published in May, 1932, two months after *A New Verlaine*. Camus devoted a whole paper to the "poet of poverty": at the outset, he quotes Rictus, cloaking himself in the poet's authority, to affirm a purpose he has taken deeply to heart and which he will follow to the letter in the brief stories that comprise *The Wrong Side and the Right Side*, as well as in certain scenes of *The Stranger:* "To make him say something at last, that someone who would be the Poor Man, one of the deserving Poor the whole world speaks of, who is always silent. That is what I have tried to do" (*Jehan Rictus, the Poet of Poverty*, see p. 116). Unable to do more, Camus makes a commentary on Rictus's prefatory statement that becomes a veritable confession: "The Poor Man walks along, sifting and resifting his misery, ruminating on his affliction. Obscure desires, sullen feelings of rebellion are growling within him. What he is thinking about, the secret of the heart that beats beneath the sordid tatters, no one knows. And yet what regrets, what aspirations are roused in him by the sight

41

of other people's happiness! The Poor Man whom everyone speaks of, the Poor Man whom everyone pities, one of the repulsive Poor from whom 'charitable' souls keep their distance, he has still said nothing" (see p. 116).

In his youthful protest, Camus, without knowing it, is taking up the cause Jules Michelet conceived when he set out writing *Le Peuple* (1846), to "assert the personality of the common people in contrast to all others." Camus contrasts Rictus's work with the dubious testimony given by Hugo, Zola, and Richepin, just as Michelet wished to disqualify those of Sue and Balzac. But how does one avoid the "academic small talk of certain modern writers" and remain faithful to Rictus? Camus leaves any minutely detailed denunciation of poverty out of his program. This he judges incompatible with the serenity of a work of art. For such exposition he waits for other, more appropriate opportunities. He will find them in joining the staff of *Alger Républicain*. As a journalist investigating the misery of the Kabyle tribes, he departs from the reserve he imposes on himself as an artist. Without transposing them into fiction, he reports "things seen" or heard: "Children in rags fighting with dogs over the contents of a garbage can" (*Misère de la Kabylie, Essais*, pp. 907–908) . . . "workers staggering, incapable of raising a pickaxe" (p. 918) because they have had nothing to eat. He bases the most vehement of indictments on this information: "Misery is not an abstract turn of phrase or a theme for meditation. It exists, cries out, and despairs" (p. 909). In closing, he endeavors to awaken the sleeping conscience of French Algerians: "If the colonial conquest were ever able to find an excuse, it would be in the extent to which it helps conquered peoples to retain their identities. And if we have one duty in this country, it is to permit one of the proudest and most human populations in this world to remain true to itself and to its destiny" (p. 938). In

Camus's case, militant journalism would not contaminate
literary creation. The young writer who in 1934 composes *Voices from the Poor Quarter* makes great efforts
not to follow his propensity for revolt or for maudlin
compassion. He keeps the memories he makes use of at a
distance. His distance is not exactly that of the witness
attempting to gain the jury's confidence. If the law of art,
as it is set forth in *Art in Communion*, demands telling
the truth and "nothing but the truth," it forbids telling the
whole truth, drawing up a complete inventory.

The obedience it demands, therefore, takes the form of
a choice. How distant still is that time to come when
Camus, aware of having given sufficient proofs of literary
rigor, will release his memory of being poor and the son
of poor people and, in *The First Man*, permit himself the
consolation of full confession! At twenty, he knew himself only through these self-imposed tasks. He gladly set
himself to transcribing into still clumsy pages only the
unexceptionable impressions that revealed to him what
he was in Belcourt, what life was, what death was, what
the mystery of mankind was. He wanted to eternalize
them by the means of Art. Put to the test by this difficult
task, his style, still groping, most often betrays him. But
the right tone is found from the beginning. To be convinced of this, one need only listen to the first of those
"voices from the poor quarter," that of "the woman who
did not think." It speaks of privileged hours during which
an odor, a sound, or a "pure emotion" suddenly weighs
upon the child with the whole burden of existence: "One
evening, in the sadness of the hour, in the vague longing
occasioned by a sky too gray, too dull, these hours return
of their own accord, slowly, as strong, as moving—more
exhilarating, perhaps, because of their long journey. In
each gesture, we find ourselves again; but it would be
futile to believe that this recognition gives rise to anything but sadness. Still, these sadnesses are the most

beautiful, for they are hardly aware of themselves. And it is when one feels them coming to an end that one asks for peace and indifference. . . . And if we were to speak about these times, it would be in a dreamy voice, as if disguised, reciting, speaking inwardly to itself rather than speaking out to others."

Camus wants to appropriate this "dreamy" voice. No thought interferes to alter the voice's testimony by interpreting it. The voice is "disguised" just as is the "very gentle" voice of Verlaine, the author of *Sagesse*, praised in Camus's article in the magazine *Sud*. It does not emit the supposed cry of the heart. It is a literary voice, which speaks "inwardly to itself rather than speaking out to others," in the manner of a recitative, the better to avoid the appearance of indiscretion. Camus does not master this art overnight. He must train the voice it has been his lot to receive. Strong, clear, well-modulated, it lends itself readily to bursts of eloquence or lyricism. He keeps strict watch over it as well. The better to control it, he lends it to characters who speak little. He even seeks to create the illusion that he has done no more than record these "voices from the poor quarter."

Actually, the voice of "the woman who does not think" is scarcely heard at all. She raises it only to protect her child from the grandmother's blows: "Don't hit him on the head," or to send him back to his "homework." Why this utter silence? Camus avoids explaining it clearly. He mentions, without dwelling on it, the mother's deafness. He evokes rather a life overwhelmingly doomed to misfortune, work, and submissiveness. A few details are enough to make one sense this: the gilded frame that holds the *Croix de Guerre* and the military medal, the shrapnel, the old woman's horsewhip, the poor woman's huddled posture in her chair, her eyes blank after a long day's work. But the experience of poverty is all the more painful because it is a child who is undergoing it. He has not reached the age of comprehension and revolt. He does not know how to sort out his feelings. He feels a strange uneasiness in the face of his mother's silence. Confusedly he becomes aware of the shame of poverty, which, though it offends justice, first of all breeds disorder in one's personal life. "He [is] afraid. He is beginning to feel a lot of things. He is scarcely aware of his own existence. But this animal silence makes him want to weep in pain. He feels sorry for his mother; is this the same as loving her? She has never hugged or kissed him, for she wouldn't know how. He stands for a long time watching her. Feeling separate from her, he becomes conscious of his suffering."*

Is this still saying too much and, above all, speaking too loud? Camus reworks the first episode of *Voices from the Poor Quarter.* Although he retains whole sentences, he tightens the preamble and omits all incidentals. The fear of giving away secrets haunts him. He is sorry to have evoked with such abandon those hours he has drawn "from the depths of oblivion" in order to record "the unbroken memory of some pure emotion"; he reduces his commentary as well by more than half. The story itself he touches less. It is stripped, however, of traits that underlined a certain resemblance between the child and the narrator: "And always the child will question himself as well as his mother. . . . He has loved, suffered, relinquished. Today he is in another room, ugly, too, and black." Camus does not wish to impose his presence nor to deform, by judging retrospectively, the "pure emotion" that remains engraved on his memory. He also avoids throwing too harsh a light on his mother's attitude. He is content to suggest the anomaly that the servitude of poverty can introduce into that most primal of human relationships, the one based on the law of blood.

* His suffering may also mean *her* suffering. See p. 245. [E.C.K.]

A last pledge to reticence and literature: the memory of the evening related in "the voice of the woman who did not think" is blended, in the final version of *Between Yes and No,* with other memories.

In contrast to that of "the woman who did not think," the voice of "the man who was born in order to die" makes itself more frequently heard. It is looking for an audience. Speaking peremptorily to three young men, it believes it has found an audience. But Camus is recording it only out of mockery. The voice begins a long rambling monologue that no one soon gives ear to any longer: "He talked, talked, deliciously losing his way in the grayness of his muffled voice." The old man's verbal incontinence provokes the same uneasiness as the silence of the woman overwhelmed with fatigue. The affliction of the poor is still incommunicable. But this time, it is associated with the idea of approaching death. If the old man no longer has anyone on whom he can inflict his repetitious drivel, there is nothing left for him but to close his eyes. This is why he tarries in the street rather than return to the "dark and dirty room" where his old woman, who doesn't wait up for him any longer and has been scornful of his homilies for a long time, will be content to say: "He's in the moon!" The anecdote, clearly, is becoming a parable. Camus plays the novelist's game less than ever. He deprives his character of birth certificate, of face, of trade. He grudgingly allots a conventional past, the "good old days" of all nostalgic types. He leads him along a nameless street. Nor is he interested in the identity of the three young men, the circumstances of their meeting, their departure. He tells his story so soberly that it becomes tragic, like the story of Apollinaire's love for Marie Laurencin, through the effect of a poetic distillation:

Notre histoire est noble et tragique
Comme le masque d'un tyran.

Poverty

Nul drame hasardeux ou magique,
Aucun détail indifférent
Ne rend notre amour pathétique.

Cors de chasse from *Alcools,* by Apollinaire.

Our story is noble and tragic
As a tyrant's mask.
No dangerous or magic drama,
No trivial detail
To make our love pathetic.

—*Hunting Horns* from Apollinaire's *Alcools.*

Voices from the Poor Quarter, an unassuming tale, certainly gains nothing in the comparison, but illustrates an equally serious wish to eliminate the "unimportant detail" that would only render it "pathetic." With the simplicity that suits such a lesson, it teaches that the experience of poverty lays bare the ignorance of youth, the anguish of old age, man's solitude in life and facing death. What better proof of his fidelity than the fate Camus will reserve for this old man by inserting him, after a few retouchings, into *Irony?*

"The voice that was roused by music," on the other hand, will be omitted in a final editing from the chorus of voices from the poor quarter that makes up the collection called *The Wrong Side and the Right Side.* This is the voice of a simple woman who tries to tell her children about her unhappiness while the phonograph plays a popular tune, "The Song of the Nightingale," whistled to orchestral accompaniment. The music's vulgarity should make the heroine's distress even more pitiable when in her naïveté she yields to emotion to the point of making confession. But the effect is merely pathetic. Camus therefore rejects it. Reading over the story of the fight between the mute brother and the poor widow's suitor, he is seized by another scruple. Doubtless he reproaches himself for transcribing too personal a memory, for threatening his own mother's dignity. Over this painful scene, too, he throws a veil that he will lift only in *The First Man*, when the risk of giving offense will, with time, have vanished. A sense of decency certainly modifies his testimony, containing it in "dikes" that raise both its moral and its literary level.

The last of the *Voices from the Poor Quarter*, that of "the sick old woman left behind by people going to the movies," will be less severely but very significantly censured before turning up again in *The Wrong Side and the Right Side*, giving this collection its tone. (*Irony*, the first story in the book, is drawn from "the voice of the sick old woman left behind by people going to the movies.") The first version is already distinctly sober. For the most part, Camus separates the essential from the incidental, the enduring from the accidental, retaining the habit of not disclosing the identity of his characters. The sick old lady has no claim on life other than her illness and her age. The narrator is only "a tall pale young man who had feelings," the old woman's only companion after the brief appearance of a sympathetic butcher's wife. The other characters remain in shadow about the family table. The daughter of the house emerges only at the moment of departure, to pronounce the closing words about forsaking her mother: "She always turns the light off when she's by herself. She likes to sit in the dark." The action takes place in a neutral décor: one divines rather than sees the dining room, the street, the house, the poor neighborhood. The story is very sparsely told: the menu of the dinner is not mentioned, nor the title of the "funny film" that everyone has elected to see.

How could one tell this story of poor people with greater poverty? Camus is still trying to achieve this when he decides to use the story again in *Irony*, for which it will be the first of three episodes. His corrections all aim at emphasizing this feature even more. He eliminates the details that underlined the old woman's poverty: "They had laid her out in an armchair. . . . She had held fast to her independence and at the age of seventy still worked to keep it. Now she lived at her daughter's expense." He refuses to indict the invalid for a spiritual poverty that makes her yield to more or less superstitious practices: why mention that Christ was on the wall, Saint Joseph on the table, the rosary in her hand? It is enough, finally, to indicate that the narrator is a "young man." He is no longer singled out by height or color. He is only a new person who discovers, without voicing it, the solitude of a worn-out human being, threatened with death, whom living persons leave behind at night.

This is how the poverty of *Voices from the Poor Quarter* becomes the poverty of *The Wrong Side and the Right Side*. Stripped of its pathetic qualities, if only by the narrative's ironic point of view, it seems to change its nature. But actually it surrenders its secret. In the course of that evening which the old woman's children will complete at the movies, time stops and space becomes empty. A scene of poverty in the poor neighborhood of Belcourt in Algiers becomes the revelation of a poverty that is absolute and universal. The poor person throws off the mask that social convention obliges him to wear. He appears as he is. He is a man like others, even more human, because he does not have the means to cheat illness, old age, and death, but submits in an exemplary manner to the common misery Pascal summarized with: "We shall die alone."

Camus knows, then, from having himself attempted to do it, how delicate it is to give a voice to man's "pain." How could he not admire the rare writers who have achieved this? He considers exemplary Louis Guilloux's "reserve," which "always prevents him from permitting the misery of others . . . to offer a picturesque subject for which the artist alone will not have to pay" (from Camus's foreword to the re-edition of Louis Guilloux's *La Maison du Peuple, Essais*, p. 1112). In *The House of the People*, what memories of his own childhood Camus finds: a family earning little from thankless work; the scarcity of money; unemployment, sickness; the smiling courage of a mother, the departure for the war of a father who will not return—the whole life of another "poor quarter"! He appreciates all the more Guilloux's manner of treating "such a subject, which lends itself to facile realism and to sentimentality" (p. 1112). The colors are so well drawn, the specifics so little stressed, that the small Breton town can become a second homeland for the child from Belcourt. Thanks to the "great art of Guilloux, who makes use of the misery of every day only in order to shed greater light on the pain of the world" (p. 1114), Camus recognizes in *The House of the People*, and even in a certain sentence that he repeats to himself with the book closed, the presence of a truth "that goes beyond empires and days: that of man alone, victim of a poverty as naked as death" (p. 1114). The class origin of the writer is not enough to explain such a success, nor is it the result of applying the principles of a more or less populist aesthetic. On June 15, 1954, a year after publishing his foreword to *The House of the People*, Camus writes to the editor-in-chief of a working-class magazine: "I do not believe that there is such a thing as a specifically working-class literature. There may be some literature written by workers; but it is indistinguishable, when it is good, from literature as a whole."* Guilloux, the son of a shoemaker, reaches "great literature" with pen in hand by conquering another simplicity. Like Camus, he invents a style for poverty. To the extent that he strips language of any superfluous ornament in

* *La Littérature et le travail, Essais*, p. 1911. [P.V.]

order to respect the eminent dignity of the destitute, he becomes classical. But it is a far cry between this kind of classicism and the one Gide cultivated as an aesthete. For Camus, as for Guilloux, understatement is not style. It is an act of fidelity.

Chapter V

The Sun

> Life is a paradise in which we all are,
> but we do not want to know it, else
> the whole earth would become a
> paradise.
>
> —Dostoevsky, *Crime and Punishment*

Will anyone be surprised that the young Camus, while
he was disciplining his voice, sometimes permitted it to
sing? In so doing, it should be said, he continued to accomplish his obligation to be a witness. Only those
"ferocious bourgeois philanthropists" he will take on in
the preface to *The Wrong Side and the Right Side*
would imagine the "poor kid" as having been an unfortunate deprived of all the joys of living. On the contrary, these joys were all the more meaningful to him
because they were few. He welcomed them without
reservation, losing not a single scrap. Camus hesitates—
because in so doing he would betray his memories—to
affirm that man's experience as a "victim of poverty" is
limited to the "pain" whose weight he bears, Christlike,
in the name of all. He willingly admits that the working
class in Europe's "chilling suburbs" is cruelly subject to
the "double humiliation of poverty and ugliness" (*Lyrical
. . . Essays*, p. 8). As for himself, at the risk of shocking
preachers of progressive charity, he clings to a secret
whose truth he is not ashamed of: "Poverty . . . was
never a misfortune for me: it was radiant with light. . . .
The lovely warmth that reigned over my childhood
freed me from all resentment. I lived on almost nothing,
but also in a kind of rapture" (pp. 6–7). Resentment is the
passion of the weak. Camus had no need to join the
Nietzscheans in order to avoid it. He was never con-
taminated. This is why poverty is linked to grandeur in

the testimony he gives of "need." The sun of Algiers shines upon the "poor quarter" just as it does on other neighborhoods. Beneath its rays, all living beings are equal. The "riches" of its light, that "true wealth" the publisher Charlot wanted to facilitate the distribution of during the prewar years, are not for sale. The people of Belcourt are their sovereign beneficiaries.

Yet, in celebrating those riches, Camus does not cease to keep the tightest rein over his language. He will strip the picturesque from his first lyrical writings just as he strips the stories in *Voices from the Poor Quarter* of their sentimentality. He does not forget that the "art" which makes up his religion must be the servant of a truth that stems no more from geography than it does from social history. But this time his fidelity finds itself exposed to more serious temptations. A whole literary style, in fact, comes from popularizing North Africa's luminous glory, as well as that of other countries that border the Mediterranean. It goes back to the success of *Fruits of the Earth*, published at the end of the nineteenth century. It was upon the oases of Algerian soil that Gide wanted literature to set "a bare foot" and make contact once more with the "earth." His songs to the glory of Algiers; to Blida, "flower of the Sahel"; and to the oases of the Southern desert evoke lasting echoes in the memory of Algeria's children. Thanks to the kind attention of his Uncle Acault, the bibliophile butcher, Camus heard these songs when he was very young. In 1935, Camus also lends an obliging ear to the "poems of African inspiration" that Montherlant includes in *Encore un instant de bonheur* (*One More Moment of Happiness*). Montherlant had extolled the lovely streets of Algiers several times since his first sojourn in Algeria in 1924; in *Paradise Still Extant* (1933), for example. Camus knew perhaps that the author of *Funeral Song for the Dead at Verdun* had dedicated all his writings to the sons of his comrades killed in the

First World War, to those "true heirs of the war" who must make certain that there will be tomorrows. If this is so, Montherlant, in evoking the emotion that seizes him as he crosses the border on the road from Fez to Algiers, moves Camus all the more: "I dream of leaping forward, of shouting 'Straight ahead!' every time I pass the road sign that divides the waters in the Moulouya River, which announces we are leaving the 'Atlantic' for the 'Mediterranean' side. . . . This is the moment when, out of sheer joy, we substitute blue ink for the black ink in our pen! Worship of the Mediterranean is not on the wane" (Montherlant, *Un Voyageur solitaire est un diable, Essais*, p. 407). As Camus's contemporaries are readying themselves to take up the literary traditions of their elders, Valéry is the archpriest of this "religion." Its dogma is set forth in his *Mediterranean Inspirations* (1933). Earlier, Valéry had outlined its liturgy. His poem *Le Cimetière marin* was recited in Algiers, as it was everywhere else. The same images and rhythms invade a similar poem, *Mediterranean*, composed by Camus in October, 1933:

> Midi sur la mer immobile et chaleureuse:
> M'accepte sans cris: un silence et un sourire.
>
> .   .   .   .
>
> De l'immense simplicité sans heurts jaillit la plénitude,
>   Oh! nature qui ne fais pas de bonds!
>
> .   .   .   .
>
>   Méditerranée!
> Blonde berceau bleu où balance la certitude,
>
> .   .   .   .
>
> Aux cimetières marins il n'est qu'éternité.
> Là, l'infini se lasse aux funèbres fuseaux.*

* *Essais*, p. 1207. [P.V.] See pp. 196–199. [E.C.K.]

The Sun

Noon on the immobile, ardent sea:
Accepts me without cries: silence and a smile.

. . . .

Plenitude springs from the simplicity, immense, unbroken,
Oh! nature which does not make leaps!

. . . .

Mediterranean!
Fair blue cradle in which certainty is poised,

. . . .

In the graveyard of the sea there is nothing but eternity.
The infinite grows weary there, from funereal spindles.

The young poet stammers, and he is too lucid not to
know the poverty of his literary means. But he feels encouraged by the example of a whole Mediterranean
literature that draws its inspiration from the very shores
of North Africa. As he would confide to Gabriel d'Aubarède in 1951, he already felt the pride of belonging to
the community of Algerian writers in French: "It is a true
flowering! The previous generation did not know how to
read. Fruit grows quickly there. It was the land of
Jugurtha and Saint Augustine, of course" (d'Aubarède,
Rencontre avec Albert Camus, Essais, p. 1342). At that
time, Camus had only friends among his countrymen.
Giving up his university career, he endeavored to make
them better known and to define their common ambition.
He became director of the Maison de la Culture in Algiers,
and forcefully affirmed in a lecture given February 8,
1937: "Our task here is to rehabilitate the Mediterranean,
to take it back from those who claim it unjustly for themselves" (*Lyrical . . . Essays*, p. 195). Camus is thinking of
[the Frenchman] Charles Maurros and his followers, ad-
vocates of a neo-classicism. As manager of the collection
Méditerranéennes, founded by Charlot in December,

1938, Camus launches the magazine *Rivages*, with the goal of "resuscitating" Mediterranean man. "From Florence to Barcelona," he writes in a presentation text that has the hint of a manifesto, "from Marseille to Algiers a whole active and fraternal people give us the essential lessons of our life. At the heart of this manifold existence, a more secret being must be sleeping, since it provides for all. It is this teeming life nourished on the sky and the sea, before a Mediterranean Sea streaming beneath the sun, that we envision reviving once more, or at least the many-colored forms of the passion for living that it causes to be born in each of us" (presentation of the magazine *Rivages*, *Essais*, pp. 1330–1331). Camus is a contributor to the *Revue algérienne*, owned by his friends the Raffis. Lastly, having become a journalist, in the book section of the newspaper *Alger Républicain* he faithfully reviews such collections of poetry, stories of a more or less romantic bent, and essays as come along to enrich the young literature of all North Africa.

But the "religion of the Mediterranean" does not make a fanatic of him. He is not a blind convert. He remains reserved amid the faithful, whose zeal seems to upset him. According to the later admission of one of them, Charles Poncet, Camus seemed "a bit distant." Was this, as Poncet supposes, a sign of the "great reserve" that served Camus more or less consciously as a defense mechanism? Doubtless, yes. Yet Camus's psychological make-up is not the only question. He determined his own attitude toward the literary vocation he discovered in himself. It prevented him from embracing the too facile career that was open to him in Algiers. In his lecture of February 8, 1937, Camus carefully warns of the misunderstanding that might distort his intentions. "It may indeed seem that serving the cause of Mediterranean regionalism is tantamount to restoring empty traditionalism with no future, celebrating the superiority of one culture over another.

. . . To us it is obvious that our only claim is to a kind of nationalism of the sun" (*Lyrical . . . Essays*, pp. 189, 190). Camus was not content with public denunciation of this kind of "nationalism." He combated it in himself, throughout his apprenticeship in the writer's craft. To submit "the play of sun and sea" to the superior demands of art, without denying their memory or altering their enchantment—what more thankless struggle!

The first serious attempt Camus makes to "fix by a constraint" one of those instants when the "true riches" of his homeland are revealed to him dates from April, 1933. He situates his illumination in a locale he knows well, just as the Tipasa of *Nuptials*, too, will be familiar to him. Often, in fact, his walks led him toward the Moorish house that was built in the Jardin d'Essai* to commemorate the centenary of colonization. It became a meeting place for lovers, among them himself. The building and its beautiful setting might monopolize a painter's imagination. But Camus was more ambitious, announcing at the outset to the hypothetical reader of *The Moorish House* (see pp. 181–192): "The restlessness that floats beneath the dome of the entryway, the confused attraction of the blue corridor, amazement at a sudden flowering of light heightening the importance of the brief semi-darkness that leads finally to the patio—infinitely wide, horizontal, perfect with light—these subtle and fleeting emotions that the first visit to a Moorish house produces, I have wanted to enlarge into more general and more human correspondences, in the presence of natural creations. I have wanted to build a house of emotions." The visitor's reverie does indeed transcend the walls between which it is awakened. It spreads freely across the Jardin d'Essai, leaves the park for an Arab cemetery, floats along the roads, moves away toward the

* A public park in Algiers. [E.C.K.]

olive orchards at Cherchell and the valleys of the Kabyle, returns, sets out again, returns once more at the will of the "correspondences" it anticipates and which its perceptions mobilize. Camus eschews, then, the role of Sunday painter, set up for the day in front of a landscape he has picked out to copy. He eliminates the picturesque again to the extent that, rather than accumulating precise details, he animates his tableaux by giving them the imprint of a quite internal movement. While night is falling, "the peace that descends from the sky is disturbed by the houses jostling one another right down to the sea, which they run up against abruptly. Their elbowings hollow out streets, blind alleyways, whirls of terraces grimacing insults to the evening calm." In the same manner, in a poem *To Celebrate a Childhood*, Saint-John Perse's hometown is stripped of its exoticism all the better to yield to the impulse that bears it toward the sea. But, despite all these efforts to strip and refine his language, isn't Camus accepting the detour of a metaphor, which, although not classical, is no less patently a metaphor? He would like to use a more direct language. Instinctively, he seeks to acquire one in recording the incoherent succession, the "sabbath" of sensations that assault him and that he has not had the leisure to master. From his vision of the little Arab shops, he wants to retain only "the invariable polychromy of the insolent yellows, the pinks heedless of harmony, the blues forgetful of good taste. . . ." These will become familiar habits later, when, as master of his art, he sings about "the sea close by." For the moment, he is trying out techniques of literary impressionism that Proust perhaps revealed to him. Only an aesthetic like Proust's responds to his wish to honor Algeria as a poor man who knows tacitly that it is beautiful, this elemental homeland that is reborn each time a child discovers the light of day. The joy of living does not make a great show of itself any more than does the "pain" of poverty.

Camus has known this by means of "subtle and fleeting emotions." He contents himself now by recalling them. It is by being faithful to their memory that he attempts to translate the deep peace that invaded him one day as he was out walking among the gravestones of an Arab graveyard above Algiers: "The day was peaceful. A mosque protected the graveyard under the fig trees. The cradle-shaped tombs roused no despairing thought, and the inscriptions were reassuring because they were incomprehensible. It was close to noon. From a terrace jutting forward, one discovered a flight of roofs ending confusedly in the blue of the sea, very far away. And the sun gently warmed the white and tender air: peace. There was no one near the graves. It seemed this calm retreat must satisfy those who were dead. The single virtue of the silence and the peace was teaching them indifference now. The eye wandered from the simple white marble, stained by the fig trees with capricious shadows, to the curly balustrade, then followed the rooftops to lose itself in the sea."

Reading this passage, which was provoked by true inspiration, reveals equally the promises and the weaknesses of *The Moorish House*. Scarcely "inaugurated into literature," Camus places himself at a distance from "Mediterranean regionalism." He writes neither for chauvinistic Algerians nor for tourists. With a great deal of discretion he evokes the particularities of the resting place the Arabs reserve for their dead; he is careful not to turn these features into curiosities. He measures his words, he shortens his sentences in order to retain the "peace" he celebrates in all its simplicity. Now and then, he strikes the first chords of that intense lyricism, dry as the cry of cicadas, that will explode in *Nuptials*. But the prelude stops short. The persistence of logical turns of phrase, the inopportune return of certain adjectives, the use of tricks of eloquence stifle the song that seeks to be sung. In the rest of *The Moorish House*, meditation will soon impose its law, as the secret does in *Melusina's Book*. How difficult it is to become poor once more with pen in hand: Camus is quite naturally tempted to show off the resources of the instrument he is beginning to use. Despite himself, he prefers himself to his subject. He conceives better than he can execute: it is the project of a discourse as transparent as the happiness of a Belcourt youngster stretched out in the sun. "I would like to have been an objective writer," he will confess in *The Enigma*. "What I call an objective author is one who chooses themes without ever taking himself as the subject" (*Lyrical . . . Essays*, p. 159). (Note: As early as 1933, in his *Reading Notes*, Camus observes, about *The Abbess of Castro* and the *Chroniques italiennes*: "They do not move me. They satisfy me. What personal objectivity! An example to propose myself." And, apropos of Gide: "The drama, the suffering of Gide, is to rediscover himself at every step. This is even apparent in his work. In his latest works he has tried to be objective: each landscape, each character is Gidian from whatever perspective it be.")

But Camus has from the first the merit to have followed that generous objectivity which is in no way related (must one be more precise?) to the platitude "descriptive literature." He does not let himself be discouraged by the imperfection of *The Moorish House*. He perseveres and he makes some decisive progress, which encourages him, in 1937, to publish *The Wrong Side and the Right Side*. The Algiers of *Between Yes and No* imposes its presence almost without detour or hedging. Camus succeeds in effacing himself before the nocturnal landscape he contemplates, seated on the threshold of an Arab café: "Is that the sound of the sea far off? The world sighs toward me in a long rhythm, and brings me the peace and indifference of immortal things. Tall red shadows make the lions on the walls sway with a wavelike motion. The air grows cool. A foghorn sounds at sea. The beams from the lighthouse begin to turn: one green, one red, and one white. And still the world sighs its long sigh. A kind of secret song is born of this indifference. And I am home again. I think of a child living in a poor district" (*Lyrical . . . Essays*, pp. 31–32). Yes, it's a "secret song" rising in the silence the writer has reestablished by lowering his voice. A few notes, which come, one would think, from an Arab flute, are enough to make it perceptible, and its rhythm is blended with the breathing of the night. . . . It is the very song of the world, whose components need not be identified (the sound of the sea?). To record it, Camus becomes once more the child from a poor neighborhood who had never stopped hearing it. He suddenly feels at home. But let no one be mistaken. The home he rediscovers is not reduced to the city of Algiers, which is, in fact, hiding in the shadows. It is the Kingdom promised to simple souls, who possess it here below because they have eyes that see and ears that hear. "But to be pure," Camus will affirm in *Summer in Algiers*, thinking of Plotinian gnosis, "means to rediscover that country of the soul where one's kinship with the world can be felt, where the throbbing of one's blood mingles with the violent pulsations of the afternoon sun" (*Lyrical . . .Essays*, p. 90). The epithalamion of *Nuptials* celebrates the union of man and the world. Throwing himself into the waves, the young Algerian receives a veritable baptism, which purifies him. Then his "legs take tumultuous possession of the waves" (p. 68), an accomplishment already sung of by Valéry in *Mediterranean Inspirations*. The swimmer exercises his "right to love without limits" (p. 68) before stretching out upon the sand, into which he collapses with "the happy weariness of a day of nuptials with the world" (p. 69). This time Camus invents a language for the happiness he knew at the same time as the "pain" of poverty, which, for him, is that of an Adam, still naked, that of the "first man."

At the moment of reaching the goal, he avoids all demonstration of a "nationalism of the sun." The *Méditerranéennes* collection would serve the cause of a literary provincialism no more than the Maison de la Culture in Algiers would submit itself to the authority of the Communist Party. There is no doubt Camus advised severity in the selection of manuscripts. Reading the works that were selected enables one all the more to taste the quality, similar to none other, of his own essays. They often compare favorably. Gabriel Audisio, when he entrusted *Love for Algiers* to Charlot, was enjoying great prestige among Algerians. Camus consulted him respectfully on November 9, 1937: "Unemployed at the moment, I have the greatest need to live in Paris. Do you think that at the age of twenty-four, with a *licence ès lettres*, a diploma of higher study in philosophy, a year of practical journalism (in editing and layout), and two years in the theater as an actor and director, I can find a job in Paris that would give me a living and time to work on my own? . . . I do not forget the spontaneous kindness that you accorded my youth and literary inexperience" (from an unpublished letter). A few days after receiving this letter, Audisio was just writing the preface to *Love for Algiers*. He declares himself therein Algerian at heart and by imagination: "I have hardly written anything," he declares, "prose or verse, for nearly seventeen years that was not more or less inspired by Algeria, lived and felt in Algeria, or in which a memory, a recollection, an allusion did not lead me back, even secretly, to Algeria" (Gabriel Audisio, *Love for Algiers*, p. 9). As one might well suppose, the praise Audisio bestows on his literary homeland will not be lacking in either warmth or color. It is loaded with happy memories, like fruit overflowing a horn of plenty: "Sometimes it is the sweetness of living, the enervating voluptuousness of balmy evenings, and sometimes it is a taste of strength, with the exaltation that new lands still eager for conquest inspire. It may be the solitude that devastates the heart atop the high plateau of Constantine, or the hustle and bustle of seafaring humanity in a suburb of Oran. At other times, it is the yearning to be a soul confronting God by searching in the sky for the Southern constellations, and at other times the wish to be merely flesh surrendering to all the modern enjoyments of jazz and big buildings" (p. 18). But the praise singer of Algeria also knows how to control his inspiration. He lets it flow in "legends" that set Ulysses and the sirens frolicking in the very harbor of Algiers. He questions it in meditations, among them one, *Pureté du Sud* (*Southern Purity*), that would not be out of place in *Nuptials*: "The purity of solitude, purity of the silence, purity of the noon sky with its blue and its sun, purity of the nighttime sky in which stars make a sparkling of lights similar to the wing-rubbings of an innumerable population of insects, purity of a gesture and a palm, purity of a shadow and a look, the purity of death itself quickly returned to the driest dust" (p. 44). Lastly he adapts his thanksgiving to reality by congratulating the new land that Algeria is for retaining such youth after a century of colonization: "Will someone say that it is paradoxical to sing of the youth of something a century old? Anyone knows that a hundred years, for the beginnings of a people, is only the interval of a few mornings" (p. 81). Camus cannot help admiring, in *Love for Algiers*, the "preposterous dancing verbal rhythm" and a certain "blend of sunshine and good sense" he will rediscover in *La Cage ouverte*. But Camus's originality sparkles in contrast. He has achieved it by refusing the easy gambits Audisio goes in for: the oratorical elaborations, the so-called Mediterranean joviality, the local color, the flirtation with mythology.

(Note: Camus censures the last severely in *Nuptials at Tipasa*: "Those who need myths are indeed poor . . . I describe and say: 'This is red, this blue, this green. This is the sea, the mountain, the flowers.' Need I mention Dionysus to say that I love to crush mastic bulbs under my nose?' " *Lyrical . . . Essays*, p. 68.) Camus clothes his very style in the "purity of the South." When he writes, he resembles the Kharijites, Islamic puritans, whom Audisio admires, but does not imitate, because he judged them to be "harsh and intolerant." In the Church, and not the chapel of Algerian writers, Camus—alone if need be—defends the Catharist cause.

Closer to Camus than the émigré Audisio are Blanche Balain and Max-Pol Fouchet of Algiers, Claude de Fréminville from Oran, Edmond Brua from Bône, Armand Guibert from Tunisia, and the person Camus venerates as his mentor since having been his student in philosophy at the Lycée Bugeaud: Jean Grenier. Fréminville, the most loyal of his companions, who bought a printing press and published the *Revue algérienne*, put out a collection of short essays, *Looking at the Mediterranean*, in the *Méditerranéennes* series. The first essay sets the grave, restrained tone: "Algiers in profile. The harbor, the bay, the factory chimneys, the Jardin d'Essai —and nothing seems artificial. There is a sort of cadence, of grave undulation of the world transmitted by a cool breeze. . . . I am amazed that men make such effort to escape from this world. . . . We are created to be men of this world. I rock in my chair. I should not like to leave it. The beautiful promise that is here. The lights and the fires of the port." Influence, or connivance? Like Camus, Fréminville is a literary ascetic. He refrains from singing of Algiers in a major mode. He grants only a few words, which he does not even bring together in sentences, to describe a site whose "cadence" alone draws his attention. It is the elemental and mysterious presence of the "world" he wants to celebrate, of this realm that has been given to man. On the beaches of his country he, too, has lived nuptial days: "There are the childlike joys of life. It seems suddenly that we are young married people, we and she, and that this is the hour of foolish pranks and games. We are infinitely good, infinitely happy. And how can one separate this communion from the one the tragic gives to us?" Camus uses precisely the same word, "communion," to designate the pure sense of being alive that it is art's function to "fix." The two friends belong very much to the same "race" that Fréminville salutes in one of his meditations, *Weight of the World*: "Here it is, our earth. Here is the belt of beings who are brotherly to me around the world. Still closer, the sea and the light that are attuned to us. A human race that does not measure itself, my race in its passionate splendor." Yet the elliptical prose of *Looking at the Mediterranean* ill serves the expression of such "splendor," merely translating glimpses of the lightning flash that will set whole pages aflame with lyricism in *Nuptials*. It is Camus who finds the right tune, nearly as distant from Fréminville's excessive restraint as from Audisio's broadness.

It seems very natural to look for his rivals among the poets. Poetry in the '30s is not the last to spread the land of Jugurtha and Saint Augustine with flowers. Max-Pol Fouchet publishes his second collection of poems, *Simples sans vertus*, in 1937; it is number three in the *Méditerranéennes* series. He opens in a humorous manner, welcoming the sun after rain, spring after winter, or pleasure after boredom:

Plic, plic, ploc, fine pluie
Trottinait sur le toit.
Ouf, ouf, ouf, soleil brille
Et d'un coup, hop! la boit.

Les copains parapluies
Vont au fond des armoires,
Animaux de la nuit
Tant ils sont noirs, noirs, noirs.

Se déplie la chenille
Endormie dans la rose,
S'éveille de nos filles
L'essaim blanc, vert et rose.

Plink, plink, plunk, fine rain
Is tapping on the roof.
Ooh, ooh, ooh, the sun
Comes out and slurps it up.

Back to the closets
With our friendly umbrellas,
Like creatures of the night
They are so dark, dark, dark.

Caterpillar unfurls
Asleep inside the rose,
Rousing our young girls
Swarm of green, white and rose.

But beneath the flippancy a personal inspiration shines
through bit by bit. Fouchet confesses to love troubles,
of which, as it happens, Camus was more than the
witness. Recalling, too, the title of his collection, Fouchet
sings of a way of life, "beyond good and evil" in contact
with the sunny sea, that he, like many other of his
comrades, believes he invented. One of his pieces, *Puisque
tout est simple* (*Since Everything Is Simple*), provides
him its theme:

Un bateau sur les flots bleus,
Une amourette au cœur,

The Sun

Faut-il plus pour être heureux,
Pour trouver le bonheur?

.   .   .   .   .   .

Un nuage dans le ciel bleu
Où se reposent les anges,
Des filles en robe bleue
Cueillent des fruits et les mangent.

Un bateau sur les flots bleus,
Des filles, des fleurs, des oranges,
Pourquoi suis-je malheureux,
Nuage où se posent les anges?

.   .   .   .   .   .

Mon ami part sur la mer,
Une voile passe sur l'onde,
A quoi bon être amer,
Arrêterai-je la fuite du monde?

A boat on the blue waves,
A lovelight in the heart,
Does one need more to be content,
To find happiness?

A cloud in the blue sky
On which the angels rest,
Young girls dressed in blue
Gather fruits and eat them.

A boat on the blue waves,
Flowers, girls, and oranges,
Why am I unfortunate,
Cloud on which the angels sit?

My friend is going to sea,
A veil crosses the wave,
What's the use of being bitter,
Will I stop the fleeting world?

It would be cruel to underscore that the poet falls short of the "simplicity" his too-smiling wisdom makes use of. What remains of that "tragic aspect Fréminville, rightly, never separates from simplicity? Or of the "secret song" Camus felt rising within him as he heard the respiration of the sea from the streets of Algiers? Fouchet's little poem sings out of tune. The liturgy of the "Mediterranean religion" calls for a heartier lyricism. It is sometimes rewarded by the spirited generosity in the work of Blanche Balain, sister of Camus and Fréminville. Born in Indochina, her poetry *La Sève des jours* (*The Sap of the Day*—1938) ripened on Algerian shores. It overflows with flowers and fruits, gathered not only in gardens, but amid the waves. It leads a bacchanalian existence in which sea and earth are united, their limbs entwined:

> *C'est vous que j'aime, mer automnale*
> *Aux vagues lourdes comme des mottes,*
> *Portant, vous aussi, mer végétale,*
> *Les grappes rouges, les pourpres hottes.*
>
> *Quand vous êtes jardin, mer fruitée,*
> *Quand vous êtes nourriture et sève,*
> *Chair d'orange, or doux, pulpe qui crève*
> *En substantielle graine pressée,*
> *C'est vous que j'aime, mer automnale,*
>
> *Vos riches paniers pour Dieux païens,*
> *Vos flots serrés en pampres luisants,*
> *Et votre fleur au cœur écumant*
> *Et votre suc épais comme un vin.*

It's you I love, autumnal sea
Of waves as heavy as clots of earth,
You, too, vegetable sea, bearing
Red clusters, purple baskets.

The Sun

When you are a garden, fruited sea,
When you are nourishment and sap,
Orange flesh, soft gold, with bursting pulp
Squeezed into substantial seed,
It's you I love, autumnal sea,

Rich basketfuls for pagan Gods,
Your billows narrow into gleaming vine-shoots,
And your flower foaming at the heart
And your juice as thick as wine.

Camus shares Blanche Balain's rapture and he likes the music that accompanies it. This is why he devotes his review in the book section for November 11, 1938, to *La Sève des jours* as he is completing *Nuptials*, which Charlot will put on sale May 23, 1939. Thoughts of his own creation are on his mind throughout the book review he is dutifully composing: "Poetry is not moving when it lacks a certain hint of the flesh to endow it with bitterness and grandeur. Every evening, men raise their heads toward the night. But when emotion accompanies this impulse of the body, lifting itself for a second to the stars, poetry is born. It comments upon, prolongs, and completes the motions that link us to the world. Poetry lies wholly in that mysterious and sensitive harmony which, from itself to us, lets love be born. This at least is true in *La Sève des jours*. But here the feeling is established in a lucid and continuous form, born of that inner fount in which order and inspiration spring forth together. . . . The secret harmony one senses between woman and nature, the interchange between the world that proposes and the soul that consents, the motion from despair to hope, from love of life to reflection over its meaning, are responsible for the emotion and the strength of these few verses." *Alger Républicain's* reviewer, as one can see, hardly bothers to analyze the merits of Blanche

Balain. Instead, he is singling out, in an ensemble of poems whose execution is far from perfect, an inspiration that he thinks is the same as that of his *Nuptials*. He knows from experience that a writer bent on bearing faithful witness must impose a "balance" on his compositions, so that they waver between "no and yes," "despair" and "hope." (Camus uses this word again in characterizing the poetry of Armand Guibert, whose book *Oiseau privé* (*Private Bird*) he presents to the readers of his column on July 15, 1939, and he uses analogous expressions in his review of Jorge Amado's *Bahia de tous les saints* on April 9, 1939: ". . . an equilibrium of yes and no, a passionate movement accompanied by no commentary.") He feels that he himself is becoming a poet, not thanks to the digression of his reverie, but to the extent to which it "follows the impulse of the body" and encloses the sensation of a "lucid and continuous" form.

If we choose to believe Camus learned this double lesson from someone else, rather than Blanche Balain, one should mention Jean Grenier. Grenier's *Santa Cruz* appeared in *Méditterranéennes* in 1937, although *Les Îles* (1933) remains his masterwork. In praising the riches of light with "simplicity," Camus is following his professor's example. He emphasizes his admiration for Grenier, one involving "neither servitude nor obedience, only imitation, in the spiritual sense of the word" (*Lyrical . . . Essays*, p. 330). Grenier reveals to Camus, first of all, how lucky his student has been to have lived since his childhood among landscapes whose purity discourages any writer worthy of the name from associating them with his own beliefs or states of soul. Grenier defines this in the preface of his *Mediterranean Inspirations*, dated July, 1939: "There is no chance of the Mediterranean causing the confusion of feelings that made the Romantics find spiritual nourishment or even an intuition of the

divine in landscapes" (Jean Grenier, *Inspirations méditerranéennes*, preface, p. 103). But, under the name of
"illumination" or "philosophical death" and referring to
the mystics of India, Grenier also analyzes a privileged
experience that Camus, in turn, had had "gazing at the
Mediterranean" at a time when poverty sharpened all
his feelings, making his joy of living the more acute.
"Then," he concludes, "you are nothing and nobody.
Not: you are *this*, I am *that*" (*Les Îles*, p. 92). At the
right moment, the prose of *Santa Cruz* is stripped to the
bone so as not to veil the "illumination" that dazzles the
wanderer, eclipsing his own person: "It is like a space
that opens but more and more widely before us, more
and more bathed with light, always more light. One
walks with rapture but with a strange rapture, which
is sure of itself and goes straight toward the goal, a sort
of embrace of Nature and the spirit" (Grenier, *Santa
Cruz et autres paysages africains*, p. 11). Thus do the
"nuptials" that Grenier, like Camus, celebrates in Tipasa
—amid the pagan temples and the Christian basilicas whose
mingled ruins lie "impartially" on the ground—announce
themselves. The desert exercises the same fascination upon
the teacher and the disciple. They intone the same song
to its glory. From Djemila, Camus's voice answers
Grenier's, who first raised his at Biskra: "The immensity
of the desert is like an abyss for the mind: the spirit is
afraid of it, refuses it, but, as soon as it begins to grow
accustomed to it, feels its attraction. . . . These pitiless
landscapes drink man up as the first hour of sunshine
drinks up the dew. . . . It sinks into the quicksand
indifferently and soon shows others only the ghost of its
true self, already united with something more mysterious
that no human language could describe. It might repeat
the mystic's words: I played at losing myself but won"
(*Santa Cruz, Un soir à Biskra*, p. 43). It would betray
their memory to make the two singers compete with

one another, like Virgil's simple shepherds. In the end, "the master," Camus affirms without the risk of being contradicted, "rejoices when the disciple leaves him and achieves his difference, while the latter will always remain nostalgic for the time when he received everything, and knew he could never repay it" (*Lyrical . . . Essays*, p. 330). The "difference" of *Nuptials* leaps to the eyes. The poor young man has made a triumphal entrance into that secret garden of art he had dreamed of while walking beside the walls of the rich estates in his hometown. He gives proof of a higher control, which, disciplining his inveterate lyricism, maintains a just equilibrium between the moment of contemplation and that of meditation. The Algeria truer than nature that his testimony finally aims at is a homeland both visible and invisible, plain and hidden, natural and mystical.

Chapter VI

The
Enigma

Yes, here Camus found his "home again." But if he is
discovering on the beaches of Algiers, among the ruins
of Tipasa, on the plateau at Djemila the harmonious land
that had welcomed the reverie of the poet who wrote
*L'Invitation au voyage** before accepting his own reveries,
Camus hardly lingers there. The miracle, or the mirage,
does not survive the "instant of eternity" it flooded with
light. It is gone in a flash. Camus does not dare to hope,
as Alphonse Lamartine did in *La vigne et la maison* (*The
Vineyard and the House*), that the Kingdom his memory
keeps fresh will be returned to him for all eternity.

Non plus grand, non plus beau, mais pareil et le même.

Not greater, not more beautiful, but alike and the same.

* Baudelaire. [E.C.K.]

On the contrary, he states, "It is a well-known fact that we always recognize our homeland at the moment we are about to lose it" (*Lyrical . . . Essays*, p. 90). Thus the Kingdom unceasingly recedes because of the Exile, the "no" keeps on challenging the "yes." The little piece of old coin that the pilgrim brings back from Tipasa has a "visible" side, with a "beautiful woman's face," but also a side that is "worn away."

By underlining the contradictions in his testimony, Camus, far from devaluing it, demonstrates anew that he gives it without cheating. He does not wish to betray either the "humble people" whose misfortune he shared or the "beauty" of the sky beneath which he was born. The ambiguity of the literary model he sets up for himself, once and for all, during his years of apprenticeship, is the measure of his sincerity. When a witness has sworn in good faith not only to tell the truth and nothing but the truth, but to tell the whole truth, he soon realizes that it is not a simple matter. And in his statements he respects the enigma that the truth becomes for him. Were he a skeptic, he might perhaps feign having a solution, one interpretation and one alone. Faithful to his promise, he accepts as his own the confession of the "adolescent" who writes *L'Art dans la Communion*: "The misfortune is that our need for unity always finds itself face to face with dualities whose terms are irreconcilable. A sort of binary rhythm, insistent and despotic, reigns over life and ideas, which may stir up more than lassitude, despair. But discouragement is not allowed. Weariness and skepticism are not conclusions. One must go further. . . ." "To go further" would mean achieving some supernatural truth, the recognition of which would resolve the contradictions of the truth at hand. The young Camus does not lightly abandon the hope of attaining this. The duplicity he believes he must show is costly. It is proportionate to the "need for unity" he

feels without alas! being able to satisfy it. He takes this
need very seriously, since he is tempted to explain
through it the fascination that death exercises upon the
living. "One might hold," he notes in April, 1933, "that
just as there is a need for unity, there is a need for death,
because it permits life to form a single block, in opposition." Could he be drawn by the mystical asceticism
whose end is to reestablish a lost unity? He does not deny
it. In a dissertation of August, 1933, on "the logic of
pre-logic," not content to applaud the mystics, "who
have made the world what it is," he reproaches sociologists for misjudging the religious impulse, defined as a
"desire for unity," in presuming to see in it only a
phenomenon of "the primitive mentality." For his part,
Camus considers that "the mystical desire for participation is a deep, mysterious, ancestral need." And he
specifies that one discovers it "at the bottom of all
thought, because participation alone abolishes the all
too real dualities and antinomies with which we struggle."
He is particularly receptive when Plotinus teaches him
that "to know the One is to be restored to one's homeland" (*Métaphysique chrétienne et néo-platonisme*,
Essais, p. 1270), and shows him the routes to that wholesome repatriation. But Pascal strikes home even more,
perhaps, with the ideas that "faith embraces several
truths, which seem to contradict each other," and that
"the source of this is the union of the two natures of
Jesus Christ" (Pascal, *Pensées*, ed. Lafuma, p. 462). Here
is a language he does not find surprising, since he speaks
it himself.

Will he abandon it in persuading himself that the light
of Revelation is refused him? One need only read Camus's
youthful writings to be convinced of the contrary. No
more than Pascal pretends to wipe away the contradictions of the human condition by ordering them about
the "*point fixe*" of the Cross does Camus dream of

reducing them by remaining an unbeliever. His "nostalgia for Unity" sharpens, on the contrary, the awareness he retains of the existence and the gravity of these contradictions. Camus makes it a point of honor to "weave from strands of black and white one rope tautened to the breaking point" (*Lyrical . . . Essays*, p. 169). He remains faithful to Pascalian doubt, a concept that applies so well to his first experience in life. Camus wholeheartedly rejects "heresy," that quite negative choice which one of Pascal's *Pensées* contains the analysis and condemnation of: "The source of all heresies is the exclusion of some [of man's] truths. . . . And it generally happens that, unable to conceive the connection of two opposite truths, and believing that the admission of one involves the exclusion of the other, they [the heretics] adhere to the one and exclude the other. . . . Now exclusion is the cause of their heresy" (Pascal, *Pensées*, tr. W. F. Trotter, p. 258).

The warning Pascal thus addresses to Camus is renewed for him, in various other forms, by several of his favorite authors. Nietzsche confirms that he would commit a "double lie" by affirming that "all truth is simple";* and exhorts him to be "rich in antitheses," for "at this cost" alone will he be "fertile." One can doubt whether Camus keeps to that last, somewhat selfish consideration. His duty to himself alone as a faithful witness orders him not to amputate the truth by simplifying it. But Nietzsche's lesson remains no less admissible. Gide takes it up again with regard to Nathanael in *Fruits of the Earth*: "The necessity of option was always intolerable to me; to choose seemed to me not so much choosing as rejecting what I did not choose" (*Les Nourritures terrestres*, I, IV, 69). And he pleads the case for inconsistency: "Inconsistency," he declares, "displeases me much less

---

* Nietzsche, *Le Crépuscule des idoles*, p. 87. [P.V.]

than a certain resolute conclusion, than a certain will to remain faithful to oneself and the fear of making mistakes" (*Les Nouvelles Nourritures*, p. 267). Certainly it seems inconvenient, almost sacrilegious, to link together here the Pascalian refusal of "heresy," which has no other motive than the love of truth, and Gidian "inconsistency," which contrasts the supposed "necessity" of "option" to the "hateful" self's desire for emancipation. Yet the two attitudes correspond one and the other to the respective "orders" to which they belong. Camus knows Pascal too well not to appreciate both the great distance that separates them and also the analogy that gives one the "corresponding number" of the other.

Doubtless he has a similar opinion of "alternation," the new virtue Montherlant justifies and defines in a text in *Aux fontaines du désir*: "To be at the same time—or, rather, to let them alternate within one—the Beast and the Angel, the life of the flesh and the body and the intellectual and moral life: whether man wishes it or not, nature, which is all alternation, which is all contraction and release, will force him to this. . . . The merit of man will be to cease to deny this basic rhythm but of blindness with regard to himself, or to forswear it for fear of inconsistency, or to apologize for it with sighs; it will be to know it and yield to it happily as if one were being cradled in the very arms of Nature" (Montherlant, *Syncrétisme et alternance*, *Essais*, p. 240). Among the models contemporary literature offers, is there another that better suits the young moralist? After it has influenced the thought of *Art in Communion*, the "rhythm" Montherlant wants us to obey is introduced as a "balancing agent" in the professions of faith in *Nuptials* and particularly in *The Desert*. (Note last portion of *The Desert*: "It is on this moment of balance I must end" [*Lyrical . . . Essays*, p. 104].) The repetition of the same words here might well be the effect of an influence.

77

At the very least, it signifies a kindred inspiration. The inspiration doubtless struck Camus when he read *L'Équinoxe de Septembre* (*September Equinox*), finding in it a new defense of "alternation." Such sentences by Montherlant might this time be drawn from *The Wrong Side and the Right Side*: "Two opposing doctrines are nothing but different deviations from the same truth; passing from one to the other, one no more changes ideals than one changes objects when one contemplates the same object from different points of view. . . . It is all yes and all no, it is the yes and the no that embrace and fuse together in time as if they will be extended and fused into eternity. All is one. And this one is good" (Montherlant, *L'Équinoxe de Septembre*, *Que 1938 est bon; Essais*, pp. 773–774). With a slight hint of religiosity, the dominating thought in *September Equinox* blends with that of *Between Yes and No*. Also, Camus defends Montherlant against the leftist press, which treats him as a warmonger because it doesn't understand his provoking rejection of all ideological Manicheism. Camus invites his readers to admire with him "one of the three or four great French writers who propose a system of life that will only seem ridiculous to the impotent." As for Camus, so well does he accept the "principle" of "alternation" that Montherlant considers as "fundamental to his life and his work" that he sets aside any univocal interpretation of *September Equinox*. No, the book is not pleading the case for war. If violence is unleashed, the righteous man who does not seek to cheat will find in some "alternate form of service" the only conduct his honesty can accept. "They divide us today into two clans," Camus bitterly observes, "according to which we choose between servitude and death. But there are many of us who refuse this dilemma, not knowing how to choose, admiring those who have deliberately stopped being active. Montherlant is not among them. But he affirms that should war come he would accept it as a sickness and within it still attempt to find reasons for living. There is perhaps no more virile passage in our literature than the one in which Montherlant affirms that he will fight without believing, without any other ideal than that of being equal to a destiny which has come without being called for." When the "plague" rages in a France occupied by the Nazis, Camus, the Camus of *Letters to a German Friend*,* was to maintain such an attitude without flinching. Montherlant would then demonstrate a lesser wish to "show respect to man" (Montherlant, *Essais*, p. 772). But isn't this retrospectively the proof that the "wisdom" in *September Equinox* remains tainted, despite what Camus says, with a certain "aestheticism"? (Note 4: "Let no one speak of dilettantism or aestheticism in regard to such an attitude. Let no one seek to present it as 'odious.' What else is it but one of the platitudes, of universal wisdom?" [p. 777].) In *The Wrong Side and the Right Side* or in *Nuptials*, the "alternation" clothes, on the contrary, that famous "authenticity" so often invoked by moralists between the last two wars. Without delighting in them, Camus accommodates himself to his contradictions. He maintains a painful equilibrium between them. Thus he subscribes neither to Pascalian "heresy" nor to that "spirit of orthodoxy" which Grenier sees as the "fatal consequence of all successful belief" (Grenier, *Essai sur l'espirit d'orthodoxie*, p. 16), but which might well, in the same manner, spoil any unquestioning unbelief.

The orientation of Camus's youthful writings reveals this bias as much as the choice of his reading matter. It can be sensed in the first text he publishes, the article

---

* Several of these appear in Camus's *Resistance, Rebellion, and Death*, translated by Justin O'Brien (Knopf, 1961; Vintage, 1974.) [E.C.K.]

titled *A New Verlaine*, from the magazine *Sud* of March, 1932 (see pp. 111–115). The Verlaine that Camus claims to free from his reputation as a "graceful fool" is a quasi-tragic poet "who prayed to God with his soul and who sinned with his mind." He calls attention to collections of poems in which "lines of repentance and those of sensual pleasure alternate." This is how *Parallèlement* can pass for Verlaine's "essential" work, not "from the standpoint of its literary worth, but of its representation of the poet's feelings." This judgment in itself would be of only faint interest. But it happens that Camus as a teenager grasps every occasion that permits him to reassert this principle, by which he has decided on the superiority of *Parallèlement*. He keeps referring to it stubbornly in his academic exercises. As to comedy and tragedy, he maintains that both are "arbitrary," since "in reality Caliban and Ariel are not separated." He recalls, apparently without thinking of the preface to Cromwell,* that "there is in man a close and moving blend of the poetical and the ridiculous"; hence the result that "there is a tragic aspect to the ridiculous, just as there is a ridiculous side to the tragic." Should he be treating a classical subject, psychology and metaphysics, he hastens to contest the unity of the actualities of awareness: "Our worst pains sometimes increase to the point that a feeling of pleasure rises from them, whether or not it is replaced by disgust and fatigue. At any moment, it is enough that one of our feelings reaches its maximum intensity for it to give rise to precisely the opposite feeling." His *idée fixe* reappears again in an exposition he must take to heart since, being ill himself, he treats in it the "two methods of medicine." He does not conceal that he prefers to the doctrine of Galen—for whom "illness is a

---

* Victor Hugo set forth a quite similar idea in this little work, almost gospel to the Romantic school of French writers. [E.C.K.]

vice that must be fought against and reduced"—that of Hippocrates, who sees illness as "a reaction of the organism against unfavorable conditions, a compensatory effort that must be helped, and sustained, rather than reduced," and that, consequently, respects the profound ambiguity of all human behavior.

When Camus learns to write rather than philosophize, the "representation of [his] feelings" conforms, with singular consistency, to the model in *Parallèlement*. To reproduce the "binary rhythm . . . of [his] life and [his] ideas," he chooses the movement of a dialogue. In the first of the *Intuitions*, *Deliriums*, and in the last, *Back Again to Myself*, the Fool, who resembles Zarathustra, engages in a discussion with the narrator, and it is plain that Camus identifies with both of them. In the same way, in *The Will to Lie*, an old man and a young man confront one another, or, in *Desire*, the narrator (once again) and an anonymous interlocutor. In *Uncertainty*, the situation is more complicated in appearance only. There are indeed three men, but the third, the narrator, has no other function than to "make peace" between his two companions, who, one learns in the end, are creatures of his imagination. How could Camus, with his bent for dividing himself in two, not turn toward the theater? The profession of acting helps him to conjure up the vertigo of "alternation" by giving him the opportunity of playing contrasting parts. The budding writer within him is tempted, in his turn, to invent a dramatic version of the "balancing" of his thoughts. He likes scenes that bring together protagonists who struggle with one another, like the exiled man from Prague in back of his shop and the man from Tipasa returned to his homeland, the man who has "death in the soul" and the one who is not "ashamed to be happy."

In *Caligula*, it seems at first that the "no" abolishes the "yes." In losing Drusilla, his beloved sister, the emperor has just learned from the school of suffering that "men die" and that "they are not happy" (Camus, *Caligula and Three Other Plays*, p. 8). He, too, is really suffering from "death in the soul." In the primitive version of the play, his despair takes the form of physical nausea: "I am sick at heart, Cæsonia. No, don't come near me. Leave me alone. My whole body feels like vomiting." (Quoted by Roger Quilliot, *Théâtre*, p. 1752. He is speaking of Scene 10, Act I, which in the definitive version of the play becomes Scene II in the same act.) The dead Drusilla's brother cannot accept the shock of death. He is deprived of the natural cowardice one of the patricians confesses to without shame: "Take my case. I lost my wife last year. I shed many tears, and then I forgot. Even now I feel a pang of grief at times. But, happily, it doesn't amount to much" (*Caligula*, p. 4). Caligula, unlike this accepting widower, refuses to avoid the fatal revelation he has had: "I'm surrounded by lies and self-deception. But . . . I wish men to live by the light of truth" (p. 9). He therefore makes his behavior conform to the "truth," as Camus made his style conform to the truth in writing *Irony* or *Death in the Soul*. Since he is supremely powerful, Caligula decides to turn the whole world about him upside down. He metes out injustice and death rather than submitting passively to the injustice of death. He becomes destiny's rival in cruelty and competes with the gods in indifference. And he explains his behavior: "There's no understanding fate; therefore I choose to play the part of fate. I wear the foolish, unintelligible face of a professional god" (p. 44). Nothing is easier for him than this, designating victims. Isn't all mankind, like Drusilla and the emperor himself, condemned to death? Dreaming of a kingdom where the "impossible" would be "king," the champion of "no" shouts out "with rising excitement": "I want . . . I want to drown the sky in the sea, to infuse ugliness with beauty, to wring a laugh from pain" (p. 16). He will push to its furthest limit—his own death—this logical reasoning about the misery of which he seeks to be both the prophet and the martyr. As he is about to strangle Cæsonia, he delivers the final word of his philosophy: "I know nothing, *nothing* lasts. Think what that knowledge means! There have been just two or three of us in history who really achieved this freedom, this crazy happiness" (p. 71).

In Camus's fable, one does not break the equilibrium of "yes" and "no" without being punished. Caligula becomes a monster. "I feel a curious stirring within me, as if undreamed-of things were forcing their way up into the light—and I'm helpless against them" (p. 15). But he does not manage to destroy the "right side of life," the will for happiness that gives the challenge to misery. Faced with the excesses of Caligula's revolt, the fragile Scipio continues to oppose it with the grace of light and promises of life. In the presence of his master, he praises the gestures, the times, the places that persuade man that his kingdom is of this world and that his exile may have an end. Actually, he, along with Cæsonia, is the only character to treat the emperor as a fellow human. His interruptions, relatively rare, question the pessimism of the one he always addresses as Caius. Why, then, is he listened to? First of all, because he is capable of understanding and loving Caligula. He was the witness to Caligula's frenzied anguish at the time of Drusilla's death. "Yes . . . I was there, following him as I usually do" (p. 5), he recalls to Cherea and the patricians. The friend of his adolescent years will never be a stranger to him: "Yes [I love him]. He's been very good to me" (p. 10). While Helicon conducts himself as a "spectator" toward Caligula, Scipio holds on to his role as confidant until the end. But he goes further. Even though life has not yet wounded him, he identifies, up to a point, with the man whose pain he understands. He explains this to Cherea, who is surprised at Scipio's indulgences: ". . . something inside me is akin to him. The same fire burns in both our hearts. . . . *I*—I cannot make a choice. I have my own sorrow, but I suffer with him, too; I share his pain" (p. 56). If the young poet ends up by withdrawing from the maniac without depriving him of his friendship, it is not because he is radically opposed to him, as the "right side" is to the "wrong side." In fleeing, he flees from the Caligula he carries within himself, he flees from himself: "I am going to leave you, for I think I've come to understand you. There's no way out left to us, neither to you nor to me—who am like you in so many ways" (p. 67).

But he is not the only one to show two faces and thus to incarnate the "alternation" with which Camus is preoccupied. Caligula resembles him more than his actions would lead one to suppose. Scipio takes on the task of explaining to Cæsonia the emperor's deeper personality, as he knew it before Drusilla's death. "He told me life isn't easy, but it has consolations: religion, art, and the love one inspires in others. He often told me that the only mistake one makes in life is to cause others suffering. He tried to be a just man" (p. 10). It is the injustice of death that has changed Caligula's behavior. He has become unjust by way of revolt, not by natural inclination or beneath the pressure of some fateful blow. To the extent that he parodies justice the better to humiliate the patricians' self-righteousness, Caligula still loves justice, with an unhappy love. He spares Scipio, who is a just man. In Scipio he rediscovered the Caligula that he was and that he remains despite his denials. Scipio is his counterpart, his harmonious image, who complements the broken image that mirrors reflect to him from that moment on. Hence the importance of the scenes in which Caligula and Scipio appear. In these Caligula conducts a dialogue with himself, with another himself. In the course of the most moving of them, at the end of Act II, Caligula becomes a poet once more (p. 37). The two fraternal foes (who are so little each other's enemy!) end up by joining voices to sing together of the "right" side of the world, of the "nuptials" of man and Nature. They are of the same race. They are communicants in the cult of a certain "purity." By the very words he puts in their mouths, Camus designates the intransigence of creatures who, knowing that their nature is twofold, just as life is twofold, cannot accept this fact. The pure choose the "right" side or the "wrong" side and not the middle ground, the golden mean, the *aurea mediocritas* of Latin wisdom. But whatever their choice may be, it does not blind them. Caligula, deciding for the "no," does not deny the possibility of the "yes." He does not confuse himself with his character in the play. He is content to play the role. This is why Camus, in 1938, thought of titling the play: *Caligula, or the Actor* (manuscript 1 of *Caligula*, from which Roger Quilliot quotes excerpts in the Pléiade edition of Camus's *Théâtre*, p. 1736). A good gambler, like a good actor, is not duped by his game. If Caligula follows rigorously the rules that he has imposed upon himself, he remembers that there are other rules, just as arbitrary and just as respectable, that permit the game of happiness, love, and poetry. Each of the two games serves the ambition that man in his misery nourishes until death, that of possessing the moon, the passion for the impossible.

Caligula's true adversaries are the patricians and the wise Cherea. The patricians are the guardians of the social system and of the wisdom of nations. Until Caligula troubles their egoistic serenity, they accept peacefully that life has two faces. They rejoice even that forgetfulness blurs death, that order reigns at the price of injustice, and, in short, that sunshine follows the rain. They are content with their lot and with themselves. They do not want to live with the cumbersome thought of man's "mystery," nor do they wish to make their actions conform to it. But their refusal is only a half-conscious one. Cherea, on the other hand, sets the bounds of studied wisdom against Caligula's tragic lack of limits. His understanding with the patricians is quite temporary. He does not conceal from them that he is not one of them. It is easier for him to talk to Caligula, and he does so very freely in the explanation scene of Act III (pp. 50–54). Like his interlocutor, Cherea knows that death is the law of this world and that man contests it nonetheless. The disagreement explodes when Cherea chooses not to live out this common experience in the tragic mode. A "reasonable fear" counsels him, "fear of that inhuman vision in which my life means no more than a speck of dust" (Act II, p. 22). Rather than aggravate, from despair, the suffering that the awareness of his misery causes the lucid man, Cherea has decided to "know where I stand, and to stand secure" (p. 51). He "wants to live, and to be happy," and considers that "neither . . . is possible if one pushes the absurd to its logical conclusions" (p. 51). His wish for a modest happiness contrasts with Scipio's poetic inspiration, as well as with Caligula's madness. Striving for mastery of his soul, he believes in ethics. Yet the humanism he professes is a far cry from the one Voltaire defends in his reply to Pascal, in the twenty-fifth of the *Lettres philosophiques*: "I conceive very well without mystery what man is. . . . Man is not at all an enigma. . . . Man seems to be in his place in nature, superior to the animals, to which he is similar by his organs, inferior to other beings, which he probably resembles in his thinking." Voltaire adapts to the situation . . . philosophically. He considers it logical, satisfying reason. "Man [according to him] is what he must be." Cherea does not share this optimism. If he condemns the "inhuman vision," he appreciates Caligula's disquieting insight. "Still, there's no denying it's remarkable, the effect this man has on all with whom he comes in contact. He forces one to think. There's nothing like insecurity for stimulating the brain. That, of course, is why he's so hated" (p. 58).

The servility of Helicon and Cæsonia represents a last version of the model Camus reproduces in creating the various characters in *Caligula*. Helicon is doomed to abjection. Yet because of the faithfulness he shows his master, he attains an unexpected grandeur. "Yes, I serve a madman. But you, whom do you serve? Virtue? I'm going to tell you what I think. . . . I've been able to watch you, you the virtuous ones. And I have seen that you had a dirty look and a poor smell, the flat smell of those who have never suffered or risked anything. You, judges? . . . You would judge someone who has suffered countless things, and who bleeds every day with a thousand new wounds?" (Scene in Act IV between Helicon and Cherea, omitted in Vintage edition of the play; in Pléiade ed., Act IV, 6, p. 89–90.) And what of Cæsonia? "The only god I've ever had is my body," she says (p. 10), and she consents to serve Caligula like a bitch. She grows vile, she executes the cruelest orders. But little by little, love raises her from humiliation. The woman Caligula strangles, in the last act, is no longer the cheap mistress who at first latched on to him. She feels transformed and she says this, maternally, to her lord, become her child: "But it's you only I'm concerned for now: so much so that I've ceased troubling whether you love me. I only want you to get well, quite well again. You're still a boy, really" (pp. 69–70). The sacrifice of her dignity and her life secure Cæsonia a sort of redemption. Her personality, in its turn, offers a "right" side and at the same time a "wrong" side. And thus the whole community of principal protagonists in *Caligula* attests that the young Camus, composing the first of his dramatic works, was still attached to the aesthetics of *Art in Communion*.

That he maintains this preference as a novelist will seem much odder. He admires a tradition of the novel that should lead him to respect the coherence of plots and above all of characters. Yet he does not submit to this tradition, because classical verisimilitude is much less important to him than the truth of his testimony, which he knows must be ambiguous. Hence the difficulties he will encounter in writing his first novel. (This is studied for the first time by Jean Sarocchi in his edition of *A Happy Death*.) *A Happy Death* was written at about the same time as *The Wrong Side and the Right Side* and *Nuptials*. Camus's imagination did not, in fact, furnish him with a complete story, leaving the details alone to be worked out, but with six episodes that go two by two. In this new project, the "right side" continues to alternate with "the wrong side." The themes of the "brilliant game," of the "House Above the World," and of the "man condemned to death" call forth respectively those of the "poor neighborhood," of "sexual jealousy," and of the "pursuit of the sun." The chapters, written either in the present or in the past, will contrast all the better with one another. . . . But won't the "binary rhythm," which once more imposes itself, block the movement of the story? Camus measures the risk. He tries, going against his inspiration, to regroup the episodes of the hero Mersault's destiny into three "parts."

1st Part.	His life until then.
2nd Part.	The game.
3rd Part.	Abandoning compromises and the truth in nature.

(Note: The successive plans for the novel are reproduced by Sarocchi in the afterword to the Knopf edition of *A Happy Death*.)

But he soon becomes aware of the price he is paying by giving the "second part" all the space it deserves. Hoping to free his imagination, which has become blocked, he sharply changes the slant of the novel. He proposes to make Mersault live a triple experiment in time: after time lost because of lack of money, time won because of the murder of the rich Zagreus; after time won, time recaptured at the seashore and on until death. Alas, his problem remains. Then, after a last attempt to improve things, Camus gives up the idea of a novel in three parts: "Rewrite novel" is what he jots down in his *Carnets* in June, 1938. And he resigns himself to distributing the chapters he has planned into two "parts."

The final result lacks harmony. The second side of the diptych, with its double surface, spoils the first. Too hastily stuck together, they seem artificially joined. Ill-rewarded for his effort and aware of its semi-failure, Camus decides not to publish his novel. His mistake was to have tied himself down to a model that did not suit him. When he thought better of it, reluctantly, it was too late; his interest was gone. Yet *A Happy Death*, even though it wears the mark of laborious composition, does not betray the principle of "alternation." The principle holds sway to the extent that Camus was obeying an inspiration more demanding than his guilty conscience as a budding novelist. First of all, alternation governs the character and the fate of Mersault. What a strange assassin! His act, perpetrated at the very beginning of the novel, makes him a brother of Raskolnikov in *Crime and Punishment* or of Ch'en in *Man's Fate*. But Zagreus's murderer is neither a monster crazed by violence nor a weak man susceptible to the torments of remorse. Camus manipulates the plot in such a way that the reader does not think of applying the law of justice and ethics to him. The man Mersault kills, an invalid tempted by suicide, had specifically instructed him that the "pursuit of happiness" makes all initiatives legitimate. He has also demonstrated that in modern society, money, lots of money, is necessary to have the leisure to buy happiness. Moreover, Zagreus, who is rich, is not in a situation to enjoy his fortune, and he has given up hope of life. Mersault, in striking him down and robbing him, therefore remains tragically faithful to his friend. He follows his example, "beyond good and evil." His victim's death was in the "natural" order. Zagreus survives in Mersault. Life continues and, with it, the adventure of a man who, despite Christ's warning, wants his kingdom to be in this world.

But Mersault would not be a Camusian hero if, on the threshold of entering Eden, he was not "struck by a vertigo that turns him away from it." To conquer the monotony of his existence, rather than settling in Tipasa, he takes the great trip he had dreamed of when he was a simple office clerk. Here he is, in Prague, in a foreign city, where the shock of death is revealed to him; where death in a sense becomes something he is consciously aware of. The time of Exile begins again. Rashly, he suddenly returns to Algeria. After having found, in the House Above the World, the most pleasant of purgatories, thanks to the hospitality of his girl friends, he retreats to Tipasa. Has the Kingdom finally been won? Yes, since he is permitted to live there and even to die there happy, a "stone among the stones." (The formula appears in the last sentence of *A Happy Death*, p. 151.) But he must nonetheless close his eyes and cease forever to decipher the "smile of the earth." The eternal halt still resembles an exile. And thus repeats itself the "balance" the young Camus imprints, whether he wishes to or not, on all his thinking, all his dreams, and all his compositions.

In *The Stranger*, nothing holds him back any longer.

The plan of the narration is wedded to the story and underscores it. It consists of two parts of equal length. The first contains one chapter more than the second (six as against five). But since the importance of his theme—the murder of the Arab—reserves this extra chapter for a place in the center of the novel, its presence at the end of the first part does not break the equilibrium of the whole in any way. On both sides, in relation to the event that tips the scale of Meursault's destiny, Camus lays out episodes that are symmetrical to one another. Their symmetry heightens the contrast between the time of freedom and that of captivity, between the reign of innocence and that of justice. Meursault's simple relating of the trip to Marengo contrasts with the reconstruction of the burial scene as it is seen by the lawyer; Meursault and Marie's happy first meeting contrasts with the young girl's visit to the prisoner; the life free of tension that the office clerk leads with his friends contrasts with the way it is received at the trial where they give their testimony. More generally, there is a radical difference between Meursault's lived experience as he records it at the actual moment and the interpretation that the examining magistrate, the prosecutor, and the attorney for the defense put on the same events afterward. The reader of *The Stranger* is invited to compare the accused's own day-by-day account with a (bad) novel, whose authors are the prosecution and the law.

An edifying comparison, if it is true that the book's "meaning lies precisely in the parallelism of the two parts," as Camus indicated in his *Notebooks* (1942–1951, p. 15). Meursault's story, because he is permitted to match the "right side" with the "wrong side," becomes exemplary. It teaches anyone who knows how to read it that a man's truth is never simple. Who is Meursault? He wears his other name, the Stranger, marvelously well. No event captures his whole attention: he follows his

mother's remains absent-mindedly. No act entirely involves him: he kills the Arab while shooting at the sun.
No one situation determines him: behind the bars of his
prison, he undertakes to relive a life that does not "belong" to him any longer. No judgment defines him:
while he is acknowledging his guilt before the judge, he
knows that he is innocent. No word is enough to express
what he is experiencing: to Marie, who asks him if he
loves her, he might just as well say yes as no. The secret
Camus slips into his *Carnets* in March, 1940, fits him: "My
home is neither here nor elsewhere. And the world has
become merely an unknown landscape where my heart
can lean on nothing. Foreign—who can know what this
word means? Foreign, admit that I find everything
strange and foreign" (*Notebooks 1935-1942*, p. 170).
Meursault, far better than Mersault, incarnates "indifference," that virtue based on the refusal to diminish
the "mystery" of man and fall into the "heresy" de-
nounced by Pascal. The examining magistrate interrogates
him desperately: "I ask you '*Why?*' I insist on your telling me" (*The Stranger*, p. 84). He obtains no answer,
because any explanation would diminish the Stranger's
"bizarreness," deeper still than those who are shocked
by it might imagine. When Meursault undertakes to
write his story, for himself and not for the public, he
does not think of justifying himself. Is he in search of self-
understanding? He has a higher ambition, modest only in
appearance, whose difficulties Camus well knew: to give
respectful testimony of his strangeness. One knows with
what scruple Camus endeavors to reproduce, as Maurice
Blanchot observed, "the very image of human reality,
when one strips it of all the psychological conventions,
when one attempts to seize it by means of a description
made only from the outside, stripped of all false, sub-
jective explanations" (Blanchot, *La Part du feu*, p. 179).
He is distrustful of adjectives, which attribute qualities to

things; of conjunctions, which establish connections; of oratorical or lyrical turns of phrase, which dazzle. Pen in hand, Meursault exhibits the same undemonstrativeness that keeps him from passing in life for an exemplary son, lover, or accused prisoner, that deprives him of the advantages of the social comedy, and that leads him, because he does not play the game that is expected of him, to the scaffold. He manages to maintain his distance from the garrulous, who have answers for everything. At the same time, Meursault relates to the simple folk among whom, like Camus, he has lived and felt happy. They are his only and his true friends. When they appear before the judges, they do not waste words. In contrast to the lawyer and the prosecutor, who go in for oratorical flourishes, they have respect for language. Céleste pays him due homage in vouching that Meursault "did not speak when he hadn't anything to say" (*The Stranger*,* cf. p. 115). But he goes even further, using to describe Meursault a word that is both the most ordinary and the most difficult to define. "They asked him," Meursault recalls, "what he thought of me and he answered that I was a man; what did he mean by that, and he declared that everybody knew what that meant" (cf. p. 115). Yes, the Stranger is a man, yet so convinced he is "like everybody" that he seems peculiar. His admissions are shocking because they are as complete as they are reserved. Allowing himself to speak of the love he had for his mother, he does not conceal that there was a contrary feeling mixed in with it. "No doubt," he declares to his lawyer, "I was fond of Mama, but that doesn't mean anything. All normal people, from time to time, have more or less wished for the death of those they loved" (cf. p. 80). He is ignorant of the usual psychology that endows the "passions of the soul" with the simplicity of chemical elements. How would

---

* Here and below, I have used my translation. [E.C.K.]

he characterize the motive of the crime he has committed? He does not recognize himself in the clearly identified character who, according to both the defense and the prosecution, after remaining dry-eyed at his mother's funeral, has shot the Arab. In relation to that person he feels like a "stranger." That is what society does not forgive him and demonstrates all too clearly. He pays for his sincerity with his life. Witness and martyr to a humanity that he strips of its supposed nature, and restores to its mystery, he is the "only Christ that we deserve" (*Lyrical . . . Essays,* p. 337).

The tale of Meursault's Passion upsets a good many literary customs. Camus not only bypasses analysis, the instrument of novelists interested in psychology, from Mme. de La Fayette to Proust, but also the "realist" technique his predecessors, from Stendhal to Martin du Gard, have preferred. He reproached André Rousseaux, author of an unfortunate review of *The Stranger,* for not having understood him. "You," he writes him, "attribute to me an ambition to be realistic. Realism is an empty word (*Madame Bovary* and *The Possessed* are both realistic novels and they have nothing in common). I never thought of such a thing. If a label had to be given to my ambition, I should speak rather of the symbol" (letter to André Rousseaux, never sent; cf. *Notebooks 1942– 1951,* p. 21). The choice of the last term somewhat distorts the truth. It seems to justify, very wrongly, the interpretation Sartre gives of *The Stranger*—in which he sees a philosophical tale, a new *Candide,* intended to illustrate the thinking of *The Myth of Sisyphus*—and, at the same time, Camus's imprudent affirmation about Sartre's novel *Nausea:* "A novel is never anything but a philosophy expressed in images" (*Lyrical . . . Essays,* p. 199). Actually, it is not an "idea" in the sense of the word intended by Vigny, theoretician of the symbol, that directs this strange work. Camus is careful not to lend the coherence of a thesis to his testimony. All philosophy and all psychology aside, he entrusts it to a narrative that takes the shape of a myth, as he will finally realize: "*The Stranger* is neither reality nor fantasy. I see in it rather a myth incarnated in the flesh of each day's heat" (from Camus's unpublished *Notebooks* of 1954; Roger Quilliot quotes this remark in *The Sea and Prisons*, p. 108).

The myth of *The Stranger*, present also but less imposing in other writings by the young Camus, from now on exercises all the power of its enthralling charm. It inscribes itself, in the manner of Melville's fables—Melville, whom Camus will call a "creator of myths," "in the denseness of reality and not in the fleeting clouds of the imagination" (*Lyrical . . . Essays*, pp. 290, 293). It is as "dark as the noonday sun and yet as clear as deep water" (p. 289). To begin with, Meursault instinctively leads the "natural" life that Rousseau expected to rediscover by withdrawing from the world. The sky and the water, even more than the earth, are enough to make him happy. At the end of the day, "the sky was green, and it was pleasant to be out-of-doors after the stuffy office" (*The Stranger*, p. 32). At the beach on Sunday, he is "basking in the sunlight, which," he notices, is "making [him] feel much better" (p. 63). But he also loves the sea when it is warm, at four in the afternoon, "with little, long, lazy waves." Venus haunts the floats then, just as in the fable. But she is a stenographer and her name is Marie Cardona. With Marie there are endless games around the buoy, kisses, embraces. After which, in Meursault's room, the two young people make love and find it sweet to "feel the summer night flowing over [their] brown bodies." Nothing, it seems, ought to trouble the regular return of dawns and twilights, the serenity of a happiness without history, lived and described from day to day. A mother's death doesn't change the order of things. Nor, although one is supposed to think the contrary, does it alter the wish to live and the joy of living of the son who is going into mourning. Life continues. And he continues to enjoy it.

Yet, from the beginning, the narration of *The Stranger* hints at a possible rupture. With his boss, with the director of the home, and with Marie—who do not ask him to justify himself—Meursault, recalling the old woman's demise, behaves, despite himself, like a man accused. What, then, is this unexpected discomfort? It anticipates a misfortune, which seems on the point of occurring during the burial, when the sun, suddenly dreadful, makes his "eyes and thoughts [grow] blurred" (p. 20), and he feels he is a stranger to everything about him. But Meursault is troubled no more than are the people of Oran at the sight of the first rats killed by the plague.* He takes up his life again without a care. The chain of circumstances and acts that are going to "lead him unrelentingly . . . toward the rendezvous that lies waiting for him" begins, without his suspecting it, with Raymond's invitation. He will note its onset in writing *The Stranger*, as the journal becomes a continuous narration beginning with chapter 5. (Jean-Claude Pariente analyzed this change well in his study *"L'Étranger" et son double*, in *Albert Camus, I, Autour de "L'Étranger,"* 1968). On the beach where he ought to be spending a very Algerian Sunday, he is, without premeditation, with five shots of a revolver, going "to destroy the equilibrium of the day." *The Stranger* would not suggest a myth if it explained this burst of violence. But the narration of the murder is only "obscure" because it reflects the brightness of "full sunlight." The noon sun: it is this specifically which is involved. Meursault has always avoided confronting it. He only came near it, reluctantly, at the end of a summer

---

* As later on, in Camus's novel *The Plague*. [E.C.K.]

morning at Marengo, while walking toward the cemetery. Now, he must face it, alone. And now the light of the sky, which ordinarily reveals the splendor of the world to him, becomes a menacing sword. He flees from it toward the shade and the stream, where an Arab stands in the way. On the blade of the knife the man has drawn, it is again the sun that shines and burns. Fire answers fire. One shot, then four echo. So many blows "on the door of [his] undoing" (p. 76).

What remains that is individual in the hero's bearing, from the moment when, deciding not to go back to the shack with Raymond, he returns to the beach? Nearly nothing and, little by little, nothing more. The thoughts, scarcely formulated, the impulses, scarcely felt, are erased. Warlike rites replace them. Meursault is called upon to commit a ritual murder. Beyond his victim, it is a God, the only God in his natural religion, that he has aimed at. He wanted to reach the Sun, father of all visible marvels, whose light blesses being: the "reddish and green earth" the "ever-recommencing" sea, deep skies, women's bodies. But if the Father is denied, his sons, men, are no longer brothers. Cain kills Abel, an Abel who has become anonymous, an Arab. And he removes himself from his people. Meursault's crazy act will surprise only the innocent, if there are any. It reflects the stubborn refusal that man, "king, but a king dispossessed" (Pascal, Pensées, ed. Lafuma, p. 220), secretly opposes to the Kingdom, because he does not have a soul vast enough to welcome or a heart big enough to accept that vertigo which has incited him to destroy what he believes he has loved since childhood.

"It is a well-known fact that we always recognize our homeland at the moment we are about to lose it" (Lyrical . . . Essays, p. 90). Meursault, in his cell, learns to love his homeland and dreams of returning to it. If he does not refuse Exile, he does not stop thinking of the Kingdom. The comedy of human justice, which pretends to put order into the life of the exiled, does not hold his attention. He has better things to do. He is looking for a proper way to "kill the time" of his captivity. He calls upon his memory, having understood that "even after a single day's experience of the outside world a man could easily live a hundred years in prison" (*The Stranger*, p. 98). He, who had lived for the moment, practices remembering. But the certainty of his coming death, after the verdict at the trial, compels him to look for other remedies. Since his imagination inconveniences him by keeping, despite himself, the hope of "an escape from the implacable rite," he finds himself a better pastime. Why, in effect, not imitate his mother, who, also certain of not having long to live, "had taken on a fiancé" (the old Pérez) and "played at making a fresh start" (pp. 153–154). In his turn, he feels "ready to start life all over again" (p. 154), and he manages to in telling the story he has just lived through, which will become *The Stranger*. Thus, at the most difficult moment of Exile, literary creation holds the power of bringing the Kingdom to life once more. It is a second birth, since it permits Meursault "for the first time . . . [to lay his] heart open to the benign indifference of the universe" (p. 154). But the night "spangled with its signs and stars" in the course of which he receives this grace, is his last. He is going to die facing the Kingdom that once more opens its doors to him. Will he step on the scaffold reconciled to this? One would like to believe so. But the challenge he hurls beforehand to the spectators at his execution is not that of a happy man. Meursault wavers between yes and no until his death.

Chapter VII

Repetition

Someone will be able to see a contradiction at the basis of all I say.
. . . Contradiction, naturally! Just as we live only in contradictions and by contradictions; just as life is a tragedy and tragedy is a perpetual struggle, without victory or the hope of victory; it is a contradiction.

—Miguel de Unamuno,
The Tragic Sense of Life

The Stranger, then, gathers into a veritable myth the "two or three" (rather two than three!) "great and simple images in whose presence [the] heart" of the child from the poor quarter "first opened" (*Lyrical . . . Essays*, p. 17). Camus's entire work reproduces with a "passionate monotony" the model of this exemplary testimony. (Camus recognizes "passionate monotony" in the greatest novels. See *Intelligence and the Scaffold, Lyrical . . . Essays*, p. 213.) His writings set forth an ideology suited to "the essential passion of man torn between his urge toward unity and the clear vision he may have of the walls enclosing him" (*Sisyphus*, p. 22). This passion, which Camus always lived intensely, has for its object the "absurd" defined in *The Myth of Sisyphus* as a "divorce" that "has meaning only insofar as it is not agreed to" (p. 31). It is "sin without God" (p. 40). After examining his youthful writings, one will understand that Camus remains obstinate but does not cheat about this drawing from the absurd, as Vigny does from the "religion of honor," the security of a paradoxical freedom. (Camus, too, is a man of honor. He writes, not without irony, in the preface to *The Wrong Side and the Right*

Side: "And yet I do need honor, because I am not big enough to do without it!" (*Lyrical . . . Essays*, p. 14). It inspires him more than ever, when, under the influence of the war and its aftermath, which lead him to make public commitments, he denounces all the century's "heresies." In *The Rebel*, Camus, to the lack of measure of his adversaries, accused of denying "their double life" (*The Rebel*, p. 305) and consequently of despairing about mankind, opposes a "rule" stretched to the breaking point between yes and no.

But how much time lost in polemics that prove nothing more than the power of ill will! Camus renews his testimony more successfully by disguising his voice. The myth of Exile that he elaborates in *The Plague* remains subject to the "balancing" of *The Wrong Side and the Right Side*. Seen up close, each protagonist reveals the "passion" that tortures him. Rieux, the doctor, is not ignorant of the fact that his treatment is "a never-ending defeat" (*The Plague*, p. 118); he maintains a "bleak indifference" (p. 83) whether in the organization or the chronicle of the struggle against the epidemic. Tarrou is overwhelmed by the thought that "we can't stir a finger in this world without the risk of bringing death to somebody" (p. 228). In the midst of the hecatomb, he feels, despite himself, a deep relief, because death, this time, falls manifestly from the sky, which he knows is "no longer the mortal enemy of anyone" (p. 228). Cottard, the pariah, who finds himself "at ease under [the] reign of terror" (p. 178) of the plague, ill conceals beneath his cynicism a frantic need for brotherhood. Grand's ridiculous foibles accentuate, in contrast, his heroic wish to "find the right words" (p. 42). Thus the conduct of all the victims of the plague attests, sooner or later, that man is, in Pascal's words, a "figment of the imagination." Imaginary also, the humanity represented in *The Misunderstanding* or *The Just Assassins*. Jan, who detests questions as much as Meursault, dies for not having spelled out his identity. Martha, daughter of a "land of shadows (*Caligula and Three Other Plays*, p. 79), where she seems comfortably settled, dreams of fleeing to sea-shores drenched with light. Kaliayev, Dora, tormented revolutionaries, are not resigned to separating justice from love. But how sharply the more or less secret lack of harmony that Camus lends all his characters explodes in *The Fall*. Clamence, "judge-penitent," ostensibly prac-tices a "double profession" (*The Fall*, p. 10). He instructs his visitors in the "discomfort" he has adopted. Like Caligula, he flings himself into "sweeping derisiveness." Yet irony is the only weapon he employs. He directs his mockery at the serious mind, which masks the "funda-mental duplicity of the human being" (p. 84). He is in furious pursuit of the falsely coherent image he was once able to give of himself. Split in two, the ironist encloses himself with his enigma in the center of his circular hell. The abjection he flaunts does not keep him from hoping, during a snowfall on Amsterdam, for the "good news" that would save the world.

From *The Stranger* to *The Fall*, then, it is still the same alternation of the wrong side and the right side. How could it not be tragic, since it deprives the man of any firm position? Discussing "the future of tragedy" before an Athenian audience in 1955, Camus defined at the same time a theater Nietzsche had taught him to love, the model of all his own work, whether literary or philo-sophical: "The forces confronting each other in tragedy" he affirms, knowing well what he is talking about, "are equally legitimate, equally justified. . . . Tragedy is am-biguous. . . . First and foremost [it is] tension, since it is the conflict, in a frenzied immobility, between two powers, each of which wears the double mask of good and evil. . . . Tragedy is born between light and dark-ness and rises from the struggle between them" (*Lyrical*

. . . *Essays*, pp. 301–303). The testimony Camus gives is equivocal because it is tragic. It is fitting to take the collected work that presents it for what it is: an enigma. In a world foretold by Nietzsche, in which "the disaster sleeping at the breast of theoretical civilization begins to make modern man uneasy" (*La Naissance de la tragédie*, 18, p. 119), it becomes a classical enigma in that it asks more questions than it answers.

Bibliographic Note

Listed below are works quoted in the preceding essay, with the exception of those by Camus, for which the parenthetical notes indicate either pages of the Alfred A. Knopf and Vintage editions or of the two-volume Pléiade editions in French.

Apollinaire, Guillaume, *Alcools.*

Audisio, Gabriel: *Amour d'Alger*, Charlot, *Méditerranéennes*, 1938.

Balain, Blanche: *La Sève des jours*, Charlot, *Méditerranéennes*, 1938.

Blanchot, Maurice: *La Part du feu*, Gallimard 1972.

Baudelaire, Charles: *Recueillement*, with "Meditation," tr. Robert Lowell, in *The Flowers of Evil*, Marthiel and Jackson Mathews, eds., New Directions, New York, 1963.

Dostoïevski, Fiodor: *Crime et Châtiment*, tr. Mongault, Gallimard, 1936.

Fouchet, Max-Pol: *Simples sans vertus*, Charlot, *Méditerranéennes*, 1937. *Un jour, je m'en souviens*, Mercure de France, 1968.

Fréminville, Claude de: *A la vue de la Méditerranée*, Charlot, *Méditerranéennes*, 1938.

Gide, André: *Romans, Récits et soties, Œuvres lyriques*, Gallimard (Pléiade), 1961.

Grenier, Jean: *Santa Cruz et autres paysages africains*, Charlot, *Méditerranéennes*, 1937.

———: *Les Îles*, suivi d'*Inspirations méditerranéennes*, Gallimard, 1947.

———: *Essai sur l'esprit d'orthodoxie*, Gallimard, "*Idées*," 1967.

Montherlant, Henry de: *Essais*, Gallimard (Pléiade), 1963.

Nietzsche, Frédéric: *Ainsi parlait Zarathoustra*, tr. Bianquis, Aubièr-Montaigne, 1946.

———: *Le Crépuscule des idoles*, tr. Albert, Mercure de France, 1952.

———: *La Naissance de la tragédie*, tr. Heim, Gonthier, "Méditations," 1964.

Pascal, Blaise: *Pensées*, ed. Lafuma, Delmas, 1960. Tr. W. F. Trotter, Dutton, 1958.

Péguy, Charles: *L'Argent*, Gallimard, 1948.

Proust, Marcel: *A la recherche du temps perdu*, Gallimard (Pléiade), 1959.

———: *Swann's Way*, tr. C. K. Scott Moncrieff, Vintage, 1970.

Richaud, André de: *La Douleur*, Grasset, 1931.

Rousseau, Jean-Jacques: *Confessions. Autres textes autobiographiques*, Gallimard (Pléiade), 1959.

Sartre, Jean-Paul: *Situation* I, Gallimard, 1947.

Unamuno, Miguel de: *Le Sentiment tragique de la vie*, Gallimard, "Idées," 1965.

Voltaire: *Lettres . . . philosophiques*, Paris, 1734.

Foreword

It seemed appropriate to have a selection of Albert
Camus's youthful writings follow an essay attempting to
relate these writings to the readings that nourished them,
and to the future works for which they served as the
model. Not all are unpublished, since Roger Quilliot
used some and quoted from others in the second volume
of his *Bibliothèque de la Pléiade* edition of Camus's works.
They do not show the formal perfection of those early
works deemed worthy of publication: *The Wrong Side
and the Right Side, Nuptials,* or *The Stranger.* Nor
does any one of them attain the fullness of *A Happy
Death.* But they reveal the dogged and secret task Camus
imposed upon himself in order to achieve a voice that
would be his alone. And they mark the advent of an
inspiration he served faithfully throughout his whole
career, of which the preface written in 1958 for the new
edition of *The Wrong Side and the Right Side* is a
powerful reminder.

The present selection is deliberately incomplete. It
contains only texts that are already coherent and fully
worked out, in which the emerging vocation of a twenty-
year-old writer is asserting itself. The order of the
presentation is chronological.

The editor is grateful to Mme. Albert Camus for her
kindness in putting all the manuscripts in her keeping at
his disposal.

—Paul Viallaneix

Youthful Writings

by Albert Camus

1932

A New
Verlaine

There is a view widely held by admirers of Verlaine, as well as by those contemptuous of him, that he remained a child, always, throughout his whole life. According to them, Verlaine did not encounter along life's way the hard and bitter experience that leads you, without raptures or laughter, toward the final end. They envy Verlaine for having remained so young, for having followed the butterfly of idle fancy without fearing to see it dissolve into powder between his fingers, for having plucked the rose of desire without fear of being torn by it. This, they say, is why Verlaine was not aware of good or evil. He sinned unknowingly. All unaware, he prayed.

That in general is what is thought of Verlaine. Yet a deeper study will show that one must distinguish two quite different aspects in Verlaine: his soul and his heart.

Studying Verlaine's soul as it is expressed in his verse, we are obliged to recognize that the generally held view is correct. This tender soul surely kept a child's freshness, a delicious naïveté, a spontaneity so moving that it touches the heart, and finally an instinctive need of caresses one can sense beneath the graceful clumsiness and the awkward charm.

But as we consider his mind, we shall see there is nothing of the child in Verlaine, nothing of the graceful fool tossed about by life. He suffered, sick in body, pained in heart. He loved, he suffered. His mind was gripped by the cold claw of experience. He was conscious of evil, and took pleasure in this awareness. Like Baudelaire (and this is only one of his many similarities to that other poet of the tender-hearted), he had a slightly cynical propensity for sin. He delighted in the thought of hellfire. He sinned in order to attract the divinity's attention, for out of pride he could not conceive of being nothing in so immense a universe; he was naïvely a believer, and if he sinned knowingly, in his soul he believed.

What I have suggested can easily be demonstrated. Let's review a little literary history. One could see, when the first selection of his verse, *Les Poèmes saturniens*, appeared, that the young and nearly unknown poet had not departed from the teaching of the masters of the day: the Parnassians. One could detect in these manicured verses the proud aridity of a Leconte de Lisle, the dandyism and insensitivity of an Heredia. Yet scattered through the book were certain lines that seemed to anticipate something new, particularly the poem entitled *Le Rossignol* (*The Nightingale*), which ended with these moving lines:

. . . *une*

Nuit mélancolique et lourde d'été,
Pleine de silence et d'obscurité,
Berce sur l'azur qu'un vent doux effleure
L'arbre qui frissonne et l'oiseau qui pleure.

. . . a

Melancholy, heavy, summer night,
Full of gloom and silence,

Lulls against the blue brushed by a soft breeze
The tree that trembles and the bird that weeps.

Then *Les Fêtes galantes* appeared; a whole cast of
characters from Italian comedy came to life, laughing,
singing, making love beneath the white light of the
moon. The accent was new. The bow of this bizarre
fiddler gave out strange and jangling sounds that
caught the heart. His book was a great success.

During this time, Verlaine led an agitated, stormy
life, which was to end in one of the greatest scandals
in literary history.

Next came *La Bonne Chanson;* renouncing his
agitated life, Verlaine became engaged, became the
tenderest, the most idyllic of fiancés:

C'en est fait à present des funestes pensées,
C'en est fait des mauvais rêves, ah! c'en est fait.

Done for the present with baleful thoughts,
Done with bad dreams, ah! done with them all.

Following upon who knows what events (for the
poet's life remains cloudy, despite the fact that he is
so close to us, and perhaps for this very reason),
Verlaine separates from his wife, falls into debauchery,
detested excesses of drink and unhealthy amours.

Repentance follows and then the admirable stanzas
of *Sagesse* ring forth, with the grave and touching
splendor of the versets in *L'Imitation*. I should like
to quote the whole of this poem, so drenched in tears,
so troubled by regrets, so touching in its humiliation,

a poem without rhyme but whose harmony grips the heart with I know not what inexpressible melancholy.

O mon Dieu, vous m'avez blessé d'amour
Et la blessure est encore vibrante,
O mon Dieu, vous m'avez blessé d'amour.

. . . .

Voici mes yeux, luminaire d'erreur
Pour être éteints aux pleurs de la prière
Voici mes yeux, luminaire d'erreur.

O my God, you have wounded me with love
and the wound is still quick,
O my God, you have wounded me with love.

. . . .

Here are my eyes, shining with error
Waiting to be snuffed out by the tears of prayer.
Here are my eyes, shining with error.

And then the lines of repentance and those of sensual pleasure alternate. Verlaine sins, then sincerely repents. Here we reach a sensitive point: Verlaine is aware of his weakness. And with a dash of cynicism, he sets faith and the taste for evil side by side in his soul. And he does it knowingly, since the poems that appear next have the meaningful title *Parallèlement* (in parallel fashion). This is Verlaine's essential work, not from the standpoint of its literary worth, but of its representation of the poet's feelings. This is the work which proves that Verlaine himself, more than any other person, was aware that he was doing wrong. This is what proves that he did not have that lovely innocence of childhood, but rather that he had that propensity for sin which is only possible in those of unusual intellect.

I have tried to explain one of the aspects of Verlaine I like. If I like him it is not so much because he created a new poetry; naïve, subtle, and fugitive, all nuance and delicacy in inspiration. It is not because his very lines are music; it is above all because he put into them his whole troubled and guileless soul. I cannot help being partial to him for his failings, for weaknesses so human as to make this delicate and wounded poet a man like the rest of us, full of cowardice and rebellion: a man who prayed to God with his soul and who sinned with his mind.

Jehan Rictus,
the Poet
of Poverty

> To make him say something at last,
> that someone who would be the Poor
> Man, one of the deserving Poor the
> whole world speaks of, who is always
> silent.
> That is what I have tried to do.
>
> —J.R.

The Poor Man walks along, sifting and resifting his misery, ruminating on his affliction. Obscure desires, sullen feelings of rebellion are growling within him. What he is thinking about, the secret of the heart that beats beneath the sordid tatters, no one knows. And yet what regrets, what aspirations are roused in him by the sight of other people's happiness! The Poor Man whom everyone speaks of, the Poor Man whom everyone pities, one of the repulsive Poor from whom "charitable" souls keep their distance, he has still said nothing.

Or, rather, he has spoken through the voice of Victor Hugo, Zola, Richepin. At least, they said so. And these shameful impostures fed their authors. Cruel irony, the Poor Man tormented with hunger feeds those who plead his case. Don't look for what he thinks, don't seek what he weeps for in the work of these speculators in poverty.

No, one among them has risen. Christ of the miserable, Messiah to those dying of hunger, he has gone forth to sow the good word. And what words! He has spoken the language of the Poor, not the academic small talk of certain modern writers, but the language the Poor use to speak to each other about eternal human suffering, a language aristocratically coarse in which pain gives rise to astonishing discoveries.

I should like to make this amazing poet better known, the poet Jules Lemaître called "long as a tear." If this modest essay could make people read him, could make him loved, I would be happy. I know that poverty sometimes spoils other people's happiness. But discomfort sometimes provokes acts of humanity, and hence may be desirable, pending something better. I am therefore going to try to analyze these anguished *Soliloques du Pauvre*.

Jehan Rictus's purpose is expressed in his prefatory poem. I shall quote two stanzas:

Oh! ça n's'ra pas comm' les vidés
Qui, bien nourris, parl'nt de nos loques.
Ah! faut qu'j'écriv' mes "Soliloques":
Moi aussi j'en ai des Idées.

. . . .

Et qu'on m'tue ou qu'j'aille en prison
J'm'en fous, j'n'connais pus de contraintes,
J'suis l'homme modern' qui pouss' sa plainte,
Et vous savez ben que j'ai raison.

Oh! it won't be the way the well-fed,
world-weary talk about our rags.

Ah! I've got to write my "Soliloquys":
Yep! I've got Ideas about things, too.

. . . .

Let 'em kill me, let 'em throw me in jail
What the hell, I can't take any more,
I'm a modern guy who's not afraid to wail,
And I'm right, as well you know.

Jehan Rictus has achieved this goal. He has given fervent expression to the morbid need of love, the thirst for tenderness that grip a man in the midst of his misery. He has expressed all the vague aspirations of the unfortunate for a haven of restful love. The homeless, the hungry, the vagabond, they, too, have hearts and souls—souls the more beautiful because they are swollen with longing.

There is really a kind of thesis in this long cry of pain, and I'll try to distinguish what it is: the *Poor Man's Soliloquies* are an expression of the Poor Man's state of soul. This miserable creature, who finds only humiliation and suffering in his earthly life, seeks an outlet for his pitiful condition in dreams. More than any other man, this one is happy only when he forgets he is a man. But, alas! harsh reality too often sends his dreams scattering, and then he is faced with the injustice of his lot, with feelings of violent revolt, alas, all too justified. There are thus two parts to the *Poor Man's Soliloquies*. There is the story of the poor devil's dreams, fantasies of peaceful universal happiness, and also the story of his rebellions. Even though these two parts are not distinct in the book itself, I believe one can unquestionably distinguish them.

I shall concentrate first, therefore, on the dreams expressed in a book quivering with pain, then on the aversions and imprecations that characterize the preacher of revolt.

First of all his dreams. Perhaps you think that this starving man dreams of feasting, that, poor among the poor, he dreams of money? No. He dreams of love. But he dreams of a love more maternal than sensual, of a love warm and protective, a soft shelter in which to rest his aching, weary limbs, the limbs of a wandering Jew of wretchedness. He dreams of a woman white and beautiful, a dream poignant in its naïve purity:

> Qui c'est? J'sais pas mais elle est belle,
> A' s'lève en moi en lune d'été,
> Alle est postée en sentinelle,
> Comme un flambeau, comme un' clarté.
>
> . . . .
>
> Qui c'est? J'sais pas alle est si loin,
> Alle est si pâl' dans l'soir qui tombe
> Qu'on jur'rait qu'a sort de la tombe
> Oùsqu'on s'marierait sans témoins.

> Who is she? I don't know but she is beautiful,
> Rising in me like a summer moon,
> She is posted like a sentinel,
> Like a torch, like a gleaming light.
>
> . . . . . .
>
> Who is she? I don't know she's so far away,
> So pale is she as night falls
> One would swear she was emerging from her tomb

Where we could marry one another with no one looking on.

Now the Poor man is deep in his golden dream, a pure dream in which he joyously rediscovers the precious soul of his childhood. He lives his dream. He forgets his fate, his condition, his hunger. "Perhaps I'll pass out when we kiss," he thinks. If he returns then to reality, to misery, a touching cry of stubborn illumination will issue forth spontaneously:

> *Ben, ma foi, si gn'a pas moyen*
> *C'est pas ça qu'empêch'ra que j'l'aime.*
> *Allons, r'marchons, suivons not'flemme,*
> *Rêvons toujours, ça coûte rien.*

> Well, my word, if there's no way
> That won't keep me from loving her.
> Come on, at it again, back to lazy ways,
> Let's keep on dreaming, it doesn't cost a thing.

A moving cry, like that of a child who doesn't want to believe his toy is broken! Ah! to meet this dream woman. She would welcome him and, caressing him, take him to bed. And he would sleep, a sleep tender and naïve, the sleep of a guiltless child:

> *V oui, dormir, n'pus jamais rouvrir*
> *Mes falots sanglants sur la vie*
> *Et dès lorss ne pus rien savoir*
> *Des espoirs ou des désespoirs,*
> *Qu'ça soye le soir ou ben l'matin,*

Qu'y fass moins noir dans mon destin,
Dormir longtemps . . . dormir . . . dormir.

Yeah! to sleep, never to open
My bleeding eyes on life again
And from then on to know nothing any more
Of hope or of despair,
Whether it's night or morning,
Whether my destiny looks less dark,
To sleep for a long time . . . to sleep . . . to sleep.

And these buried dreams usually have spring awakenings. The Poor Man suffers at the happiness of others. Down pathways that vanish into darkness, among hedges in bloom, the sight of shadows in tender embrace fills his heart with a nameless sorrow. He, too, would like to love; he, too, would know how to speak of stars and flowers. No, it is not a complicated love he needs, but a love that will be content with bunches of violets at forty cents each.

This great sad dream of naïve love is accompanied by another. His poverty, his anguish lead him to hope for better times. And his childish beliefs well up: what if Jesus were to come again, he who was poor, who was born in the hay, who suffered to redeem his brothers? What if the red-haired one "with the heart greater than life itself" were to come again, he who said: "Cursed be the rich!" And once again he is carried away by sweet dreams. And the Poor Man lives his dream. He sees the Gentle One with the dreamy eyes. And now a shining fantasy overwhelms him. The Poor Man meets Jesus or believes he meets him. The scene is unprecedented. The Poor Man asks Jesus for an explanation, shows him how he has failed. Ah! yes, he has failed. They've put Jesus on the stage, in verse, in an operetta. "You've become a marionette, a puppet." The Poor Man pities Jesus, who seems thin and pale. And how sincere his final exclamation! He addresses the Church, all the make-believe devout, and asks them for a bit of bread: "Some bread for Jesus Christ, who is dying of hunger!"

Then comes a long confession. The Poor Man opens his heart to the gentle Jesus, pours forth all his distress. He tells him of his own naïve beliefs. Is there no longer anything in Heaven?

> *Sûr gn'a pus rien! Même que peut-être*
> *Y gn'a jamais, jamais rien eu.*

Sure there's nothing more. Perhaps there
never even was, never was anything there.

And anger shakes the Poor Man. He insults a Jesus with no power to relieve the miseries of this world:

> *Ah! je m'gondole! Ah! je m'dandine!*
> *Rien ne s'écroule, y'aura pas d'débâcle.*
> *Eh! l'homme à la puissance divine,*
> *Eh! Fils de Dieu, fais un miracle.*

Ah! I shake with laughter! Ah! I rock with it!
Nothing is collapsing, there won't be any crash.
Hey, man with divine power,
Hey, Son of God, make a miracle.

The day comes when the Poor Man perceives that
the man he was insulting is only himself pressed
against the window of a wineseller's shop. And the
philosophical conclusion of painful resignation is
reached: "Telling people off's a waste of time."

What is more beautiful than this dream! Ah! Jesus,
weep! Your "bank of love is bankrupt":

Ton paradis? la belle histoire
Sans être vach' de réalité.

Your paradise? . . . Big deal!
Tell me another!

Sad, sordid, ragged, and haughty, the Poor Man goes
his way, scorning the impotent God.

Destitute, he feeds upon these dreams, quenching
his thirst at the fountain of his illusions. But harsh
experience sometimes yanks him back to reality. And
anger leaves him shaking. But, alas! his rage is useless.
Even though he says: "They disgust me, these people,"
even though he talks from time to time about "bump-
ing off" the first passer-by, his child-poet's soul re-
covers its self-control. And helpless, hestitant, unhappy, the poor man speaks to God.

The song entitled *Prière* (*Prayer*) is but one long
appeal to the supreme hope. The Poor Man tells God
the story of his lamentable life, a painful confession:
it is springtime. The Poor Man, suffering from hunger,
weeps also for love. And he asks God why his lot on
this earth is the worst. His is man's eternal lament:

Quoi y faut dir'? Quoi y faut faire?
J'ai mêm' pus la force de pleurer.
J'sais pas porquoi j'suis sur la terre
Et j'sais pas porquoi j'm'en irai!

What's to say? What's to do?
I ain't even got the strength to cry any more!
I don't know why I'm on this earth
And don't know why I'll leave it!

He refuses to suffer. He is weary, weary of economists and legislators, weary of kings and masters, weary of parliaments, popes, and priests. He wants to be happy. He wants it with all his being. He wants to live, even if it should mean living like an animal.

Car au printemps, saison qu'vous faites
Alors que la vie est en fête,
Y s'rait p'têt' bon d'être une bête
Ou riche et surtout bien aimé.

For in spring, that season of yours
When life's a celebration,
It might be good to be an animal
Or rich and, above all, beloved.

Thus hopes and disappointments endlessly succeed each other. The eternal conflict between Dream and Reality. Asleep in a doorway, the Poor Man is still, always, dreaming. He marries, his simple dream of love is realized, but a brutal passer-by wakes him with the threat of prison. And once more it is the stumbling walk toward who knows where, with dragging feet, empty head, body stiff with cold and hunger. Lost in his dreams, in his illusions, this is the rambling path of the Poor Man. A dreadful cry of revolt flung at the world's face.

.   .   .   .

This, I believe, is what one can see in the works of Rictus. But the best and most penetrating of analyses could not render the emotion and the sadness that emerge from this book. Moreover, to analyze a masterpiece like this is perhaps to defy Art. One should not analyze true and sincere works. That sort of literary dissection kills emotion. I have attempted here the sincere review of a sincere book.

What is most winning in these pages is the contrast between the Poor Man's dirty, muddy life and the innocent blue of his soul. It is that he has kept the candid soul of childhood. Despite his suffering, he still believes in pure love, he has held on to his child-like beliefs. His illusions, great and simple, are still intact. Let us not undeceive him.

Illusions like these one admires and envies.

The Philosophy
of the Century

I was eagerly anticipating the work that was to be Bergson's crowning achievement. Bergsonian philosophy was a question, it posed a problem. The answer was missing. With the birth of this book came the reply. It disappointed me.

Bergsonism, actually, was much more a treatise on method than on knowledge. It was a defense of direct knowledge, of intuition. It pleaded the case for the "immediate givens" of our awareness. It also cautioned against the dangers of analysis; that is to say, against reason and the intelligence. It was, finally, a treatise on an instinctive philosophy. There is nothing more attractive than this idea: to set the intelligence aside as dangerous, to base a whole system on immediate knowledge and raw sensation. Its effect was to define all the philosophy of our century. This anti-rational philosophy is latent, actually, in many great minds of our time. The idea, then, was fine. But Bergson merely proposed it. He demonstrated all the advantages of intuition. He proved one could have confidence in instinct. He emphasized the dangers of the intellect. In a word, he constructed the method and all the elements of a philosophy based on the instinctive. Thinkers, on the other hand, were ready for it. Desperate for action, the century adopted the instinctive method, became imbued with Bergsonism. The philosophy encountered no opposition except from philosophers themselves. Most literary and cultivated people welcomed it.

Rightly, then, we were expecting an effective application of the method. What was there left to do? Everything and nothing. Nothing, because since the method had been well defined, its application ought to have been automatic. Everything, considering the immense role this philosophy ought to have played once applied.

The philosophy was awaited and ought, in fact, to have been able to play the role of religion in our century. People expected a kind of ethics or completely instinctive religion that would be like revealed truth. They anticipated a sort of scripture invented by the intuition, which should have been understood intuitively. All those who had accepted the Bergsonian domination of instinct over the intellect would have accepted this scripture. What greater destiny could Bergson have dreamed of for his philosophy? A religion of the century, for it would have released and translated religious views latent in contemporary minds. A religion Bergson might have offered to his time, certain that it would be followed with a fine instinctive outburst—one of those explosions of enthusiasm that sometimes demonstrates the secret domination of the instinct over the intellect.

This, at least, is what I had dreamed of. His philosophy seemed to me the most beautiful of all philosophies, for it was one of the rare ones, along with Nietzsche's, that denied everything to Reason. And I was also anticipating the sublime conclusion of a long series of brilliant works.

The Two Sources of Morality and Religion disappointed me. Not that Bergson is not still, in this volume, the fastidious writer and acute philosopher we knew him to be. But he has not fulfilled the great role I had hoped he would. Everything along that line still remains undone. Certainly he is still making the case for intuition and putting the intellect on trial, by showing us that religion is nature's defense mechanism against the power of the intellect, stifling to the individual and detrimental to society. Bergson's is still the philosophy of intuition when he shows us that the truly religious are mystics, because their belief is instinctive and not reasoned. But we already knew that instinct could render the whole truth. We all knew the advantages of the intuitive method. We were simply waiting for its consequences.

Why has Bergson not simply communicated these results to us? Why did he not create a masterwork instructing us in the truth? What a magnificent conclusion for his philosophy that would have been!

Instead: some analysis to demonstrate the dangers of analysis, some intelligence to teach one to mistrust the intellect, some fabulation in order to create the idea of fabulation, and, throughout, such oppositions as these. In truth, Bergson finds perpetual contradiction in himself. How can so intelligent a being set himself up as the enemy of the intellect? When he makes use of intelligence in order to prove the danger of intelligence, we still accept the method as, in a sense, homeopathic. But there is something close to disappointing—or rather, something irritating—when he uses the method and abuses it in order to demonstrate the applications of the philosophy.

From this viewpoint, then, Bergson has not completed his work. Everything remains to be done. While he is still nonetheless an admirable philosopher, the man's great age does not give us much hope of seeing him accomplish what we so much desire. But perhaps another philosopher will come along, younger, more daring, declaring himself Bergson's heir. He will make Bergsonism an established thing, and then move on to its immediate realization. Then, perhaps, we shall have the philosophy-religion, that gospel of the century, for want of which the contemporary mind grievously wanders. Is this, in truth, too much to ask?

Essay on Music

The aim of the present essay is to show that music, because it is the most complete of the arts, must be felt rather than understood.

It is important to define clearly at the outset our manner of conceiving Art. Two great theories are currently held: Realism and Idealism. According to the first, Art ought to concern itself exclusively with the imitation of Nature and the exact reproduction of Reality. This is a definition that not only demeans Art, but, further, destroys it. To reduce Art to a servile imitation of Nature is to condemn it to produce only the imperfect. The greater part of the aesthetic emotion, in fact, is a product of our personality. The beautiful is not in Nature; it is we who put it there. The sense of beauty we feel before a landscape does not come from the landscape's aesthetic perfection. It comes from the fact that the look of things is in perfect agreement with our instincts, our propensities, with everything that makes up our unconscious personality. This is so true that the same landscape seen for too long a time, gazed at too often, ends by being wearisome. Would that happen if it carried its own perfection? The greater part of an aesthetic emotion is therefore produced by ourselves, and Amiel's saying "A landscape is a state of the soul" will always be true. Moreover, if we posit that the arts are reduced to the imitation of Nature, if we admit that certain of them, like sculpture or painting, may achieve some adequate results, it is nonetheless true that with others—like architecture and, above all, music—this would be impossible. That Nature expresses harmonies proper to musical inspiration is certain. But do we say that Beethoven or Wagner is limited to imitating them? What advantage, besides, would we gain from these necessarily unfaithful reproductions of Nature? Nature itself would much more surely produce a clearer and purer aesthetic response.

We shall therefore consider the realist thesis as indefensible. And, furthermore, what poor works it has given birth to! For one Flaubert, how many Zolas?

What, then, will our conception of Art consist of? It is not exactly the idealistic school's, which, while it quite rightly opposes Art and Nature, sees the merit of the former in what it adds to the latter.

This idealist theory too often transforms itself into moral theory, stimulating works that are flat, false, and boring because they want too badly to provide examples that are healthy, respectable, and destined to be imitated.

For us, Art can be neither an expression of the Real nor an expression of the Real embellished so that it is falsified. It will simply be an expression of the ideal. It will be the creation of a Dream World attractive enough to conceal from us the world in which we live with all its horrors. And aesthetic pleasure will reside exclusively in the contemplation of this ideal world. Art will be the expression, the objectification of things such as we feel they ought to be. It will be personal and original basically because the ideal, for each of us, varies. It will be a key opening doors to a world inaccessible by other means, where everything would be beautiful and perfect, beauty and perfection being defined according to each one of us. And we insist on the role reserved for personality in Art. An ugliness that is personal is worth more than plastic beauty, which is pure imitation. "What the public reproaches you for, take precious care of; it is you," Jean Cocteau said.

It is upon this initial conception that we shall build. We shall rely on two theories—or, rather, on two thoughts—Schopenhauer's and Nietzsche's. Nietzsche's, in any case, derives directly from Schopenhauer's despite some divergences of which we will make note, remembering that where aesthetics are concerned Schopenhauer is inspired by Plato.

First of all, we shall set forth Schopenhauer's theory, which will allow us the better to grasp its influence on Nietzsche's. We shall, moreover, accord a larger place to Nietzsche, first because he devoted a considerable part of his work to art, and also because this poet-philosopher's strange personality is too magnetic not to deserve first rank.

From the exposition of these two theories, we shall attempt to draw some conclusions as to the value and the role of music.

Schopenhauer and Music

Before speaking of Schopenhauer's theory about music, it may be appropriate to give a rapid summary of his general philosophy. This should help us to understand some of the tendencies of his aesthetic, by showing the close connections between that aesthetic and his theory of the Will.

Just as Leibniz wished the whole Universe were Thought, Schopenhauer, inspired by Buddhism, declares the whole Universe is Will.

Thought? "An accident of the will" peculiar to the higher animals. Will is at the bottom of everything. The Universe is only an arrangement of wills acting like forces. Everything is Will and the Will creates all: the animals' organs of defense and attack as well as their means of nutrition. The root stretches out in the earth and the stem reaches upward toward the heavens only through Will. Even minerals are full of obscure inclinations and strengths. We define these forces as weight, fluidity, or electricity, but in reality they are manifestations of Will.

For Schopenhauer the Will is something extra-intellectual that cannot be defined with clarity and logic. One can consider it, in short, as the irrational principle of all life.

All these latent wills vie with one another in strength, making the world a perpetual field of battle. Schopenhauer can therefore declare frankly—agreeing here, but only here, with the Gospel—that life is not worth the trouble of living. Pleasure does not exist— or, rather, it is negative. It results from the satisfaction of the will, and since will is eternal, pleasure disappears as soon as it is experienced, in order to make way for some other need. All our efforts are directed toward one goal, which, no longer attained, disappears to leave us once more with a new emptiness, a new need.

All our efforts are sterile; we cannot create. The only goal we can achieve is to "realize will." All human existence is directed to this end. And in order to attain it, there is but one means: Art. This is what Schopenhauer is saying when he states that Art is only the "objectification of the will."

This general philosophy allows us to understand Schopenhauer's theory of aesthetics:

He studies Art from a metaphysical point of view in relation to the Platonic "World of Ideas." For him, the special knowledge that reveals this "World of Ideas" to us is Art. The origin of Art is the knowledge of Ideas, its goal is the communication of this knowledge. Art is one of the means offered the soul for eluding the grip of the Will, of Life.

For Art, Time and Space no longer exist. Art detaches the object of its contemplation from the rapid course of phenomena. And the object, which was nothing but an invisible molecule in the dull and uniform flux, becomes in Art the great All, the infinite plurality that fills Time and Space. It stops the wheel of Time, for only the Idea, stripped of all earthly attachment, constitutes its object.

According to Schopenhauer, what we call beautiful are objects not subject to the ordinary principles of Reason. Art is the contemplation of things independent of Reason. Beauty has no rational cause. This is how Art may be contrasted with those other forms of knowledge, which are grounded upon experiment and produce Science. Artistic impressions are grouped and clustered together in such a way as to form a sort of screen between Reality and our awareness. Then alone does "the Represented World" become separate from the World of the Will; that is to say, then alone does the World of Ideas become separate from Life. The sole end of Art is to shape this felicitous prism. And when it has been accomplished we have a vague feeling of deliverance.

From this general theory, Schopenhauer draws a series of particular consequences:

Genius is no more than the most perfect objectivity, and the principal role of genius is to "fix in eternal formulas what fluctuates in the haze of appearances." And for this the genius must abdicate all social personality and completely ignore his interests, his will—in short, his life.

From this theory as well, Schopenhauer also draws his too famous comparison between genius and madness, which, he says, in one respect touch and penetrate each other. Indeed, madness is never anything but a disorganization of the memory. The madman, while having very exact notions about his present, imbues his past with incredible fantasy. And it is conceivable that in the case of insanity caused by great sorrows, Nature has sought to rid the madman of a disappointing past, just as we dismiss some disagreeable idea with an automatic gesture of the hand. In the same way, Schopenhauer says, our sense of the sublime resides in the contrast between the idea our Will gives us of our smallness and the feeling of our elevation above the concrete, a sense pure knowledge gives us.

Moreover, in architecture, beauty springs from the contemplation of a contrast between resistance and strength, on the one hand, and matter, on the other. In sculpture, to attain the Beautiful, the sculptor should not copy Nature, but should bring out the Idea it suggests.

Schopenhauer's pessimism leads him to see tragedy as the highest form of Poetry. And the tragedy will be all the more perfect the better it represents misfortune as a natural and daily event.

As one can see, Schopenhauer's doctrine on artistic matters is in a general way contrary to Naturalism and Realism. And to interpret it in a simple way, we shall say that Art is contrasted to Reality in order to make us forget Reality. And this will be echoed in Wagner's music, an incarnation of Art's purifying action. Indeed, the important thing for the artist, in Schopenhauer's view, is to create an illusion so perfect and so attractive that the spectator or the listener not only cannot invoke his Reason but will not wish to.

But the most radical consequence that Schopenhauer draws from his system is in favor of Music:

Only one art fully fills its function: that is Music. Music is completely outside the hierarchy of the other arts. It is not even that Music is superior to the others; it forms a world apart. Music does not express Ideas. It is expressed by the Will, parallel to these very Ideas. It expresses the essence of Will. It manifests that quality fleetingly before it is completely individualized. And, Will being the first cause of life, Music is the very rhythm of Life. But it expresses neither ugliness nor suffering. Indeed, serious music cannot make us suffer. Never will a musician be able to touch the reality of Life itself. Music, by the simple fact of "being," thrusts aside all that is troublesome or wounding. It can, certainly, induce a gentle melancholy in us, but since we seek this melancholy as a blessing, can we say that it expresses ugliness and suffering?

But Music is nonetheless the very rhythm of Life, a delicate rhythm that wards off all pain. We can in fact easily make a parallel between Music and the World:

The fundamental note, whatever it may be, considered as the simplest individuality of Music, will then correspond to raw substance; and the scale and its successive gradations will correspond to the gamut of the biological species, ascending in perfection. And finally Melody, which is to Music what line is to a drawing, will correspond to conscious will, the basic element of life. One cannot deny that Melody is indeed characterized by an infinitely rapid series of impressions, which, linking and coordinating themselves in our mind, allow us to attain an ideal World above Reality.

And so, according to Schopenhauer, Music is a World apart. His conception is clearly opposed to Naturalism and Realism, which would, in short, reduce Music to the cult of imitative harmony.

We have kept for the end one essential remark: for Schopenhauer, Music cannot be born of non-musical ideas, while, on the contrary, it is the absolute essence of Music to evoke in the listener the activity of visual imagination. This remark has its importance, for it is, above all, on this point that Nietzsche will be distinguished from Schopenhauer.

We can now determine the three chief points of Schopenhauer's theory: Music expresses the absolute ground of things and of life. Musical ideas do not derive from non-musical ideas. It is the essence of musical emotion to evoke sentimental images in the listener, and this is one of its seductive elements.

This is what is essential in the philosopher of the Will's aesthetic theory. We shall not examine it, for the best critique that can be made of it lies in the exposition of Nietzsche's ideas on the subject. Nietzsche, a very respectful student indeed, was also a very independent and very disobedient disciple. Carrying Schopenhauer's ideas to extremes in one of his works, Nietzsche at the same time rejected some of them in another of his works.

Nietzsche and Music

We think it useless to examine here Nietzsche's general philosophy. It is too well-known. We might even say that it has been too ill-understood and too ill-interpreted. Although it consisted of only a single burst of generous vitality, people quickly accused it of egotism. One must add that it seems at present to be appreciated at its fair value.

We must remember, however, that if Nietzsche was strongly inspired by Schopenhauer, setting out from the same point, he nonetheless worked out a complete reversal of Schopenhauer's values. Both take suffering as their base. But whereas Schopenhauer worked out a democratic ethics, Nietzsche arrived at an ethics of aristocracy, that of the Superman; whereas Schopenhauer came to sterile pessimism, Nietzsche reached an optimism based upon the rapture of suffering.

Let us examine this point. For many, Nietzsche is indeed an optimist. But, to express a personal opinion, I would say that in reading his books one might wonder whether such beautiful and poetic appeals to redemptive suffering do not conceal a soul fundamentally pessimistic but refusing to be so. There is, in fact, something frantic in his stubborn optimism. It is a sort of perpetual struggle against discouragement, and this is what we have found most attractive in a figure otherwise so strange.

What could support this opinion of ours is Nietzsche's immense pride. Like a hard shell protecting his sensitive poet's and artist's nature, a pride worthy of respect because he paid for it with his solitude.

We said earlier that there were two aspects to Nietzsche's aesthetics, one proceeding from Schopenhauer's ideas, the other, in contrast, refuting some of these ideas. We shall now present the first and more important aspect, discernible above all in *The Birth of Tragedy*:

Nietzsche sets out from the natural tendencies of man (typified in his work by the Greeks) to arrive at his conclusion. It is surely undeniable that we take pleasure in dreaming, that we enjoy living an imaginary life a hundred times more beautiful than reality. This is because we feel the need to forget our individuality and to identify with humanity as a whole. This is what Nietzsche calls Apollonism; that is to say, the need to metamorphose Reality through Dream; the sort of ecstasy symbolized by the ecstatic Apollo. At the same time, we are driven by another instinct, symbolized by Dionysus, the god of disruptive, emotional life. The Dionysiac instinct plunges us into veritable rapture and its effect is to make us forget our own individuality. Together, these two instincts combine to make us forget what is painful in our existence. The Greeks, more than any other people, felt these needs, and one can, according to Nietzsche, distinguish two tendencies in their genius. At first they tended to plunge into Dionysism and then to call on Apollonism in order to control the initial movement. After a long age of organized orgiastic ceremonies—during which participants, possessed of sacred delirium, like such elemental beings as satyrs or nymphs, would abandon themselves to sensual frenzy—the Greeks had to make an enormous effort to dominate the Dionysiac need for rapture and enchantment, to arrive at something purer and more ideal. The reason was not, as has for too long been thought, their need for perfect ideality. The need to create serene beauty, Apollonian beauty, is due above all to the sense of human pain, much more deeply rooted among the Greeks than among other peoples.

"The Greek conception of beauty emerges from pain." This is the basis of Nietzsche's theory.

Apollonism and Dionysism are, in fact, a consequence of the need to flee too painful a life. The

Greeks were torn by political struggles, ambition, jealousy, all sorts of violence. But, you'll say, it is the same for other peoples! Yet the Greeks, because of their sensitivity and emotivity, were more prone to suffering. They felt the horror of their life much more cruelly and were thus fatally destined for Dionysian barbarity. The need to remedy uncontrolled terrors called for the creation of forms—or, rather, dreams— more beautiful than those of any other people.

And to create these forms the Greeks made use of music and the dance. They disciplined mystical frenzy by means of cadence. They also created an art equally satisfying to the imagination and the feelings. They created tragedy as well.

As we have seen, the root of Greek thought is a bitter pessimism. (What is more pessimistic than the Greek maxim: "Happiness lies in not being"?) Because of their disposition for dreaming, however, the Greeks were able to forget life. They did not seek to make life more agreeable; they annihilated it through Dream. For existence they substituted beauty and rapture. So Greek serenity came to be. And what Schiller calls "Greek naïveté" was not naïveté at all. It was above all the ability to make life disappear and to dream: the only mode of existence is Apollonian and, consequently, life is but an illusion. The Greeks have always recommended that life be disregarded. They used to punish cruelly those who wished to know: Socrates had to drink the hemlock.

Thanks to dreams, therefore, the Greeks avoided despondency. For their whole attempt was to extract from suffering a "will to triumph." Only Music can express this effort to live, this anguish in the face of life.

Music indeed gives us primitive feelings in a pure state. It brings back the feelings of those fauns who danced madly about Dionysus. (Dance externalizes these feelings.) When the Greek choruses danced, Music and the Dance made them forget all individuality. The actor lived intensely the personage he incarnated. Caught up in this sort of collective madness, the spectators accepted the illusion, making no further appeal to Reason. A new state of mind emerged through the hypnotic effect of Music.

They no longer saw Dionysus in his suffering, but in his glory and his radiance. Dionysus became Apollo. This is true of the tragedies of Sophocles and Aeschylus: in place of Dionysus, there is action, which in the beginning takes the form of a simple dialogue. The heroes of the play are nothing like real men, and the proof is that they cover their faces with masks, and wear buskins on their feet. Inordinately tall, wearing false faces, they no longer have anything in common with other men. They are, says Nietzsche, manifestations of the will to live.

This long analysis of *The Birth of Tragedy* was necessary to show how Nietzsche came to his first conception of modern music, a thoroughly Schopenhauerian concept, which would lead him to praise Wagner's art.

It is undeniable that Greek tragedy later declined, when the Greeks sought to substitute reasoning for enthusiasm. Socrates with his "Know thyself" destroyed the Beautiful. He killed the beautiful dream with his evil need for rational debate. Socrates had to be condemned. Science and philosophy replaced the surge toward the ideal. And Nietzsche, by the same token, attacks the rationalism of his time.

What, then, was Music to be? Music and Myth are twin forms of philosophical redemption. Let us explain why:

Nietzsche establishes a comparison between Ancient Greece and his time. What happened in Greece might very well have happened again in the nineteenth century. The way to escape from the withering rationalism of the time was to refashion the tragic soul within us. According to Nietzsche, tragedy had to be born again. Through Myth, a new state of the collective soul had to be created that would accept a new illusion. The blindness of the Will and that inner surge toward the Beautiful had to be re-created. Tragedy would be reborn with the Renaissance of Music. For the anguished lament of the rationalist soul, Myth would substitute ecstasy before the Apollonian smile. Music, closely tied to Myth, would then be metaphysical. Philosophy, like modern science, had clumsily torn the veil from salutary illusion. Musical drama would weave this veil anew and create the Renaissance.

It is clear that in this aspect of his thinking Nietzsche subscribes wholly to Schopenhauer's theory of the metaphysical nature of music. For Schopenhauer, we know, ideal beauty coincided with the indeterminate, and this is essentially a metaphysical idea. We shall now briefly set forth the second aspect of Nietzsche's ideas. We shall then see how the first aspect, just described, would necessarily lead him to see Wagnerian art as the apotheosis of Music, while the second part, in contrast, would drive him to do battle with Wagner.

In fact, Nietzsche was developing at the same time some opposing ideas in a little work: *On Music and the Word*. While he had recognized elsewhere that the great role of Music is to create a Dream World that makes us forget the present, in this treatise he rejects Schopenhauer's thesis, according to which musical emotion must necessarily suggest feelings and images. We say "suggest" and not "start out from" feelings or ideas. He said that if we enjoyed Music because of the feelings it inspired in us, the visual images it suggested to our mind, then we ran the risk of not understanding Music at all. In order to enjoy Music purely, one had to appreciate its very essence, one had above all to enter into the analysis of harmony itself. This is a far cry from ecstasy, rapture, and enchantment. Won't the act of analyzing Music destroy its charm? Does Reason, then, no longer destroy the Dream? That the technical aspect takes priority is certain, but only in producing harmony. But to say that one can only appreciate Music technically is to say, like one of our contemporaries, that one cannot enjoy the beauty of a tree without knowing that it is made up of cells and fibers.

It is only possible to understand these contradictions in Nietzsche's work—clear and blinding as they are—when one remembers that he is a poet as much as a philosopher, and consequently liable to fall prey to numerous contradictions.

What would remain in Nietzsche's mind was the second aspect of his thought, and it was partly because of this that he deliberately broke with Wagner. The latter's completely metaphysical Music could not accommodate the intrusion of Reason. "Enamored of Wagner, Nietzsche collided with the Wagnerism that went with him." Yet Nietzsche's first conception of music had led him to defend Wagner's Art. In his musical dramas Wagner had indeed united Apollo and Dionysus, Poetry and Music. At first Nietzsche saw in that art a possibility of regeneration for Germany. The flowering of this most intense of arts fired him with enthusiasm.

The history of Nietzsche's relationship with Wagner is too well known for us to dwell on it. Yet the break so marked Nietzsche that it is impossible not to recall the reason for it. The philosopher of the will to live was as excessive in his friendships as he was prompt to destroy what he had adored. But each of his disillusionments embittered Nietzsche's already unstable character a little more. The break with Wagner was a hard blow. One cannot emphasize too strongly the misunderstanding on which their friendship had been based. Founded on error, it could not endure.

Rapturous over *Tristan and Isolde*, Nietzsche saw Wagner only as the inspired author of this shimmering drama of love. He saw in Wagner only the extraordinary means of reaching his own goal, the regeneration of Germany through musical drama. In deifying the musician, he had forgotten the man.

In his *Renaissance of Tragedy*, Nietzsche had given Wagner the superb and colossal role of Germany's redeemer. Hypnotized by the role, Nietzsche forgot that the man filling it was human, capable of all weaknesses and vanities. The disappointment was harsh. He saw his idol's vanity and weaknesses clearly. The final blow was Wagner's conversion to Christianity. Nietzsche's god had found himself a master. From this moment on, Nietzsche saw all the flaws in Wagner's art. Unjustly, because he had discovered Wagner the thinker was a bore, he scorned Wagner the musician. Like Nietzsche, to be sure, we consider that Wagner's art is blemished by his symbols, his thesis, in fact his libretto. But Wagner will be eternal because his music is pure music. That Nietzsche would not recognize. He broke his idol and shattered it to pieces. The misunderstanding was over. Inspired by the second aspect of his thought, Nietzsche would violently attack Wagner in his pamphlets. The break with Schopenhauer came at the same time as the one with Wagner.

That is the essence of Nietzsche's ideas on Music and their consequences. From his and Schopenhauer's philosophies, we are going to try to draw some personal conclusions as to the definition and the value of Music.

An Attempt at Definition

Music can, in short, be considered as the expression of an unknowable world, a world of spiritual essence expressed in an ideal manner. There is nothing indeed, more ideal than Music: there is no form—or, rather, there is no tangible form—as in painting or sculpture.

And yet each piece of music possesses its own individuality. A sonata, a symphony, is a monument just
as much as a picture or a statue. Beethoven's quartets
possess their own easily grasped architecture, a model
of perfection. There is one specific element of music's
attraction: it expresses the perfect in so light and so
fluid a manner that no effort is necessary.

Music is the perfect expression of an Ideal World,
which communicates itself to us by means of harmony.
This World unwinds, not below or above the Real
World, but parallel to it. A World of Ideas? Perhaps,
or perhaps a World of Numbers, since it reaches us
through harmony.

Why does it reach people? Plotinus can give us an
answer in his admirable theme: the Beautiful, an Idea
among Ideas, cannot be attained except by the person
who contains this Beauty in himself. It cannot be
attained by anyone whose eyes are obstructed by "the
yellow mucus of vice."

And the proof that Music comes from an unknowable world is that if a musical phrase can evoke
completely personal feelings and images in us, a feeling cannot evoke in us a musical image.

Let us explain. One way to enjoy Music is to let
a whole world of images arise within us when we
happen to hear a phrase we like more than others.
Literary memories and those with mythic qualities,
personal memories, above all, blend to form a special
and composite world in which we take pleasure. A
sort of sloughing off of the intellect occurs. This explains the interpretation of famous symphonies and
sonatas. Interpretations, moreover, that are altogether

arbitrary, since one can and ought to fashion one's own according to one's own inclinations. Every interpretation will thus bear the original stamp of its maker.

Music then can arouse in us feelings of every sort. But the visual images in poetry and literature, on the other hand, cannot evoke musical images—that is, specific images. A poet like Verlaine, for example, may give us the vague impression of musicality. But ordinary feelings cannot awaken in us distinct musical phrases. Which proves our thesis. This would indeed show that between this world and the world in which Music originates there is no common denominator. The irreducibility can only be the one that exists between the known and the unknown. Although as we hear a musical phrase we can easily imagine a ray of sun piercing the clouds, the spectacle of clouds letting this ray shine through will not in itself evoke in us the slightest musical sensation.

One could multiply such examples to infinity.

The obvious reason is that though it is possible to construct something new out of something known, it is, on the other hand, impossible to translate from the unknown through the known. This is why Music is not a language. To consider it so would be to lessen it. Or, if you wish, it is a language that can be translated into another, but not the obverse.

Music, which arouses feelings in us, is sometimes seriously accused of being purely evocative and reduced to a sort of means of recalling agreeable sentiments.

This objection has been advanced primarily by

Pierre Lasserre, who sees in it a means of destroying Schopenhauer's theory. We do not believe the objection is well-founded. We acknowledge that if Music limited itself to awakening certain agreeable images in us, its role would be singularly reduced. But Music is not limited to that. Certainly it causes all sorts of feelings to rise within us, whether literary or purely personal. But Music does more: it allows us to create an entirely original world that we construct within ourselves using images and feelings evoked as raw materials. In this way we create something new with something known. This is the only form of creation of which man is capable. To be sure, he invented imaginary animals and beings, but by combining raw materials from this earth; a centaur is a mixture of man and horse. An angel has wings. A dragon is always the composite of various animals. One cannot conceive of Paradise without a door.

Thus it appears that the unknown can only be created with what is known. And so with Music. The criticism sometimes made of it is therefore baseless: Music is as creative as it is evocative.

We can affirm, then, to summarize, that Music is the expression of an unknowable reality. This reality makes do with a single translation, the most beautiful and the noblest of all. The translation, Music, allows us to form, with the feeble elements at our disposition and by the route of our imperfect minds, an ideal world, which is particular to each one of us, which differs from one person to another. There is something of this in the Hindu theory that makes the world the product of our desires.

Now what will the value of music be?

First of all, it will be a means of reaching a state of ecstasy permitting us to forget the world in which we live. Music will allow us vertiginous evasion, a rapture—temporary, perhaps, but real. With the possibility of living in a purer world, free of pettiness—made for him, created by him—man will forget his vulgar wants and his ignoble appetites. He will live intensely that life of the spirit which must be the goal of all existence. The fauns danced around Dionysus, torn to pieces by the Titans, danced until they were possessed by an ecstatic rapture, danced until they forgot their individual selves and were no longer anything but elemental creatures, danced until they saw Dionysus no longer in his suffering, but in his glory and his radiance.

Like those fauns, like all those who by means of any rapture forget their lives in order to throw themselves into another, more attractive, we make use of Music as if it were a potion, in order to achieve the sacred rapture that will fling us into a Dream World, making us forget the World of Suffering. Everyone recognizes this magical effect. Let us recall the passage in Dante's *Divine Comedy*, where Dante, descended into Hell, meets a singer who has been very famous in his time. He asks him to sing. Hearing him sing, the spirits stop, captivated, forgetting the place in which they are, forgetting that there one must "*lasciate ogni speranza*." And so they remain until their pitiless keepers come to get them.

Musset was very true and very profound when he

said jokingly, "It's Music that made me believe in God."

Now more than ever it would be good to speak, with Nietzsche, of a music with redemptive qualities. Music brings a new bloom to the rationalist and systematic minds of our era, to feelings that have been shriveled by unscrupulous ambition. A spiritual redemption, yes.

Ordinary people, like intellectuals, feel the need of a music that suits them. It is a manifestation of the metaphysical need we bear within us: a need that makes us thirst for an Ideal Realm, thirst to forget this too material world. Music helps us forget all that is murky and ignoble in our existence. It permits us to arrive at that beautiful "ancient innocence" which consists, as we have seen, of the ability to plunge into dream in order to forget the present. And we cannot find anything to express this better than a comparison with what Jean Cocteau, in *Les Enfants terribles*, calls "playing the game." That is to say: the half-awareness into which children plunge, dominating Time and Space and initiating dreams. Music brings us a similar ecstasy. An ecstasy that seems made for beings superior to us since men weary of it. How often, actually, do we not emerge from a concert dead-tired! So much emotion has exhausted our imperfect nervous system.

Consequently, like the Greeks, who feel more than any other people the pain of their life and give themselves to dreams, abolishing all sense of the present, we ought, in order to forget the cruelty of this world—a cruelty we feel acutely because of our civilized sensibilities—to plunge ourselves into dream; and in order to do that we must call upon the only art that allows us such oblivion: Music.

In concluding this attempt to define Music, we could examine what its relationship is to the other arts: painting, sculpture, architecture. We could in principle establish a hierarchy of values in which Music would occupy the summit. Music is the most perfect art. It has been said it forms a separate world, for it alone has achieved the highest Beauty. The other arts, despite all efforts, do not seem to have achieved a Complete Beauty. Thus a great moat separates the domain of Music from that of the other arts.

Further, when we examine in greater depth the goal of each art, it would seem that what Painting and Sculpture have, above all, strived for is, like Music, Harmony.

Painting obviously seeks the harmony of colors. This is not its only aim, but it is important. And this is what made the slightly tardy but certain success of the Impressionist school, which, by the division of tone, obtains such dazzling effects of blending and harmony.

Sculpture seeks the harmony of shapes. In ancient statuary, what then were the canons of Praxiteles if not the measurements that permitted one to establish exact proportions between the different parts of the human body? Architecture itself seeks simplicity and harmony of lines. And this is why Greek temples and monuments are among the most beautiful, for they have united simplicity of shape and harmony of line.

In spite of everything, these efforts toward harmony

have not achieved perfection, because these arts met with an almost insuperable obstacle: matter.

Music, because it does not need to vanquish matter and above all because it has a completely spiritual foundation, a mathematical substratum, has achieved perfection and made harmony its very essence.

This is what explains the irreducibility of Music into the other arts. This is what explains why it constitutes a world all its own.

Yet we believe that although there are great differences of degree and means between Music and the other arts, there are no differencs of essence.

In any case, one thing will always bring them together: that is their goal.

All the arts can be identified as arising from a common yearning of the human spirit for a better world of forgetfulness and dreams.

Conclusion

One may have noticed that in the foregoing we sided with Schopenhauer, resolutely detaching ourselves from the aspect of Nietzsche's aesthetics that contradicted the philosopher of the Will. In truth, this aspect of Nietzsche's thought is problematical. Indeed, it contradicts absolutely the thesis he had set forth in *The Birth of Tragedy*, his most characteristic and most important work. One will object that it is nonetheless on these same dubious ideas that he leaned in order to attack Wagner after *Parsifal*, but we have already seen that before he attacked Wagner, a disagreement had arisen between them. And one can believe that following the misunderstanding, Nietzsche grabbed the first argument that would allow him to do battle with Wagner.

Accepting only the theory set forth in *The Birth of Tragedy*, there is no doubt that we do not share his feelings in the "Wagner Case" and "Nietzsche versus Wagner." If only Nietzsche had been able to continue ignoring the man's character in order to focus on the composer's genius, he would have understood that his aesthetics had been realized in Wagner's work. By his very subject matter, Wagner leads us into Myth. We know very well that all Wagnerian mythology reeks of the affected and the false. But it is nonetheless true that this mythology can make us dream. False and artificial though it be, just the same it can bring us forgetfulness. Nietzsche would also have understood that in Wagner more than in any other musician the union of Myth and Music was realized, and in music that is metaphysical. He would not then have treated this music as decadent. And above all he would not have compared Bizet and Wagner. Music must be "Mediterraneanized," he said. That is to say that everything in the Greek soul that favored dream was also necessary in music.

Why, then, go in search of cold Bizet, some of whose bravura arias have so greatly aged, in order to contrast him with a Wagner overflowing with lyricism and tenderness, who has remained and will eternally remain young?

The very fact of comparing *Carmen* to *Tristan and Isolde* already testifies to what we affirm—that Nietzsche, disappointed by the character of the man, unconsciously sought pretexts to attack the composer.

For anyone who conceives of Music as we do—that is to say, as a means of dispensing forgetfulness—Wagner will be one of the rare composers who fully realize the ideal. Above all, Reason must be banished from Music as from all art. Enough of musical acrobatics, of *Water Fountains* or *Gardens in the Rain*, which beg for analysis in order to unravel the composer's intention. An exception must be made, however, for Stravinsky. But notice that if pastoral imitations, farm noises, the lowing of cattle, and so forth, abound in this composer, they all lead to the same end, the communication of the soul of a country. In this, Stravinsky's work belongs to folklore and also to mythology, which brings him back to our theory.

In general and in conclusion, truly fertile Music, the only kind that will move us, that we shall truly appreciate, will be a Music conducive to Dream, which banishes all reason and all analysis.

One must not wish first to understand and then to feel.

Art does not tolerate Reason.

Intuitions

I have wished to be happy as if there were nothing else for me to be.

—André Gide

These reveries were born of great lassitude. They record the desire of a too mystical soul, in search of an object for its fervor and its faith.

If they are sometimes despondent, it is because there was no one to accept their ardor. If they are sometimes negative, it is because no one wanted their affirmations.

But despite the errors, the hesitations, the tedium, and the lassitude, the fervor remains, ready for super-human communications and impossible deeds.

1. Deliriums[1]

When the fool came into my bedroom, I was very sad. I was sad because I did not know what I wanted to be, all the while feeling very acutely that I did not want to remain what I was. I was looking for the meaning of life, of that life I did not know.

It's then that the fool came into my room and said to me:

"You will never be happy if you continue to search for what happiness consists of. You will never live if you are looking for the meaning of life. In the same way the most fertile emotions will be lost to you if you insist on analyzing them.

"Listen[2] to my madness.

"Not knowing is the mark of a fortunate[1] state of mind.

"Knowing, which is usually considered a step in the right direction, is only an enslavement of the mind.[2]

"Refusing to know is an emancipation, a definitive step in the right direction, and a liberation of the soul.

"Watch how I behave.

"I live by refusing to know that I am living. I do not discuss the vain problem of death or the soul. And I am happy because I do not try to reach happiness by seeking out its elements."

Provoked by these bold assertions, I said to the fool:

"But your position with regard to life rests on a theory. Isn't that theory a problem? What else are you doing at the moment but engaging in discourse on the subject of life?"

And the fool replied:

"I told you all that because for a moment I abandoned my madness in order to make you understand me better. But once out of your room, I'll be myself and I'll behave like a fool. I shall live without knowing it. Right now, I am able to divide myself in two: I know that I am the fool. But in a few minutes I won't know anything. My mind will no longer elaborate on things. It will make recordings.[3]

"Just the same—if today I divide myself in two on purpose—there are days when this happens to me in spite of myself.[4] Then I am weak and cowardly. At such times,[5] I am like you.

"But that's nothing. I still want to confide to you the secret of my happiness. I am the fool and I love with a universal[1] love. Your unhappiness comes from the fact that you still do not love fully. You are weak and all weakness requires love. I'm afraid moreover that even when you love you ask for reasons why you love."

And the fool was right. I would have preferred him to be wrong. He was looking at me and in his eyes I saw the flash of universal love. He loved everything. He accepted everything. He loved me at that moment.

I closed my eyes in order not to know that universal love in my turn, no matter how little I might know it. I did not want to burn and I stayed very much alone in my room, holding on to my weakness and the voluptuous enjoyment of my weakness as my only consolation.

I waited a long time for the fool. I needed only his presence. But he did not come and I consoled myself with the thought that he lived intensely and that he was happy.

Yet one day[2] he came. He was sad and weary, and I understood[3] that he was suffering one of those states[4] of depression he had spoken to me about.

He said to me:

"I do not always think the same, but this morning I have an enormous wish to be like everyone. I would like to have a wife and children, to earn my living, to have a name and the respect of good folk. But I am forced to realize that this wish is a sign of originality, one madness more. . . . You understand my torment." The madman was very gentle. He walked about the room. Stretched out on my bed, I listened and watched him. I liked him very much at that moment.

"Besides," he began again, "I suffer over that as I suffer over every contradiction. Within myself, I reconcile everything. I am the Conciliator. It remains evident that I cannot destroy external contradictions. They are the essence of life itself and I am impotent before them. This is why my torment is incurable. I see, for instance,[1] in your library the books you prefer:[2] they teach you to scorn books. That is inconceivable."[3]

"Perhaps it's because of this contradiction that I like them," said I. The fool became scornful:

"Don't think that paradoxes will give you originality. Trust in common sense."

I remembered then that he yearned to be like everyone else—a long silence.[4] The fool spoke thus:

"I am thinking of these contradictions, I am dreaming about life, and I am desolate, for dreaming about life is still living. I wander in this impasse and meet other wanderers who, like me, envy those who do not think and drink the sun in over there, in long draughts."

I, in my turn, spoke and I said:

"There is nothing to be done against intelligence. Any revolt is impossible."

"Yes," said the fool, "if one remains among the ordinary. But you have just made me see my stupidity

in seeking to be like everybody. I can only forget
my intelligence by being myself. Also why analyze,[1]
why rebel? Isn't living rebellion enough?"

Although I was used to such sudden changes, I could
not help laughing, and he cried out delightedly:

"You see, laughter ought to be our sole preoccupa-
tion. But I know not what degradation is attached to
laughter. For man a feeling—love, hate, sacrifice—is
beautiful only if it is bathed in tears. Isn't it absurd?
Suppose it pleases me to hate while laughing?"[2]

And the fool spoke again:

"My happiness, you see, is in my ability to forget.
You recognize this as I do. That is the truth I must
teach mankind."

And he left.

Wearied,[3] I watched him leave. I admired his youth
and his love, but I had not the strength[4] to behave
the same way. The call of my future, the painful pre-
occupation with forgetting my past: these were the
concerns I was turning over in my mind.

And the fool strode off with great footsteps; he went
out to join other men. And, finding them, he brought
them together and spoke to them thus:

"I am neither weak nor strong. I am nothing, for
I do not know myself, having forgotten myself. I am
happy and I come to bring you the good word. I come
to tell you: Forget yourselves.[5]

"You wander mournfully, and for some of you
unhappiness comes from the fact that you know your

weakness, and for others because you know the uselessness of your supposed strength.

"You created art in order to have forgetfulness. Unfortunately, the Artist sees in the work of art only a means of reviving his wounds.

"Men, you suffer only because you are yourselves. Forget. There are a thousand ways to forget. The earth, the sky, Dreams, action, God, everything[1] is an object of love.[2] Love life in its multiple forms. Love it for itself and not for what it reveals in you. And to start with, love me. As I love you.[3] I am the fool and that is all. I am the Universal because I do not want to be individual. My life and my happiness consist of closing my eyes to the elements of my life and my happiness. Communicate in life and in love."

But[4] men locked the fool up, for they held on jealously to what made each of them a particular human being,[5] and were afraid to renounce it.

But from his prison the fool continued:

"God does not know himself. This is why he is God. He created the world in his delirium and forgot it.[6] And I, too, have been made divine by the ability to forget. Listen to me, men. Believe in my madness.

"Any religion, any ethics, any education that affirms you in your sad individuality is bad. Create the Universal. Fashion your religion. But do not give it a name.

"Men, do not believe in your originality. And you whom I love, you the weak, my brothers, forget that your weakness wishes to parade itself.[7] Forget the weakness that seeks the pleasure of being itself. Nothing counts but the present moment, which stamps out everything, the life that is past and the life to come."[1]

Then people killed the madman, for they held on jealously to what made each of them an original being, and feared to renounce it.

But death could not reach the fool, for he had set it at a distance by refusing to know life.[2]

And the madness rose from his body.

I was watching the people pass by beneath my window when the fool came into my bedroom.

He said to me:

"What are you looking at there? Leave those stupid animals alone. I've just left them. I spoke the truth to them and they remained deaf. I offered them happiness and they refused it. I abandon them. But I still have you. Together we discovered the truth that I, in my stupid generosity, wanted to give people. Together we shall live this truth. And, Gods at last, we shall have[3] perpetual desire."

The fool was right. I looked at my detested room. I looked up at a very pure corner of the sky. Slowly I shook my head and said no, for I, too, am a man.

The fool will live alone, then, and alone he will expand his precious truth. He is scornful of me and he is right.

.   .   .   .

When will the audacious dawn of my resolutions rise up for me? When will I have the courage no longer to be a man?

Men who have broken their chains sail toward faraway islands, tasting the pungent skies and the vigorous splendor[1] of the sea breeze. They do not look back, disdaining the cowardly wake that flees from the propeller and dies.[2]

Où donc est la vraie vie, heureuse,
puisqu' elle n'est pas l'attente?

Where then is the true, the happy life,
since it lies not in anticipation?

2. Uncertainty

The music had stopped and the two men were silent. There were colors on the walls. And a bright morning laughed behind the windowpanes.[3]

One of the men got up and shook off the torpor the music had plunged him into. But the torpor was made of personal feelings and passions, and it became plain that it did not wish to go away. The man lifted his shoulders and sat down,[4] discouraged, to take up his dreaming once again.

But the other man was not dreaming. He was thinking. And so it was he who went to open the windows. An odorless golden vapor rose from the garden. The morning was free and easy. The man breathed in the light air deeply.

Quite alone in my corner, I watched them both without curiosity. The music had made me sink into the void of spiritual impotence.

Yet[5] in our respective indifference I sensed a drama.

The man was still framed in the window. He was looking out. Things were bursting so with life that one might think they were surrendering their secret. It was then he spoke:

"I am made to give orders," he said, "because I know how to limit my desires. The finite and the relative of this world content me."

The man who was seated smiled uneasily and made a defensive motion. But the other was already speaking again:

"I despise those who say that they are made neither to obey nor to command.[1] For they are made to obey while grumbling about it. There is a freedom that consists of giving oneself and binding oneself."

As for myself, I did not find it surprising that the man spoke without transition of such lofty[2] things. And my indifference persisted. I had been given so many formulas for happiness, systems of life, and religions that nothing of the sort moved me any longer.

But the one who was seated spoke:

"You are right," he said, "but you are only right. For myself, I am weary, horribly weary. Weary of searching for truth and happiness; weary of setting a rule of conduct for myself that I do not observe; weary of everything, incapable of seeking and of acting, feeding on my lassitude. My need for the infinite is wasting away by dint of living. I am one of those who say that they are made neither to obey nor to give orders. I am one of those who obey, grumbling as I do so."

He did not even weep. And without being afraid I

observed this wreck who was feeding on the pleasure of being a wreck. I had probed and contemplated myself for too long not to take great satisfaction in being a spectator.[1]

Yet I realized that I was looking for myself in these two men. But I saw that both of them were looking at me. And I thought it was fair for me to speak in my turn, since both of them had spoken:

"What I might say, everyone has said before me. And there is not a single position with regard to life that has not already been taken. I am not weary. I am not strong. I want to be unconcerned."

And I stopped, smiling,[2] happy with my life, aware of the tormented and mystical state of my soul. In so doing, mentally and with force I repeated to myself the word: "lie." And the word, which at first had been very meaningful, became flat and blurred with the repetition, so that little by little I lost myself in its emptiness, fixedly[3] repeating syllables without any meaning.

These states of obliteration are a habit with me. At moments like this any effort at intelligence becomes extraordinarily painful. But when I roused myself this time:

Everything had disappeared. I was alone in my room, and I went on wearing myself out in vain attempts to make peace between the two men I had created and to make peace between the past that haunted me and the freedom I was hoping for.

3. The Will to Lie

The world was as it is every day. There was neither a special breeze, nor a violent wind, nor an extraordinary calm. And we did not notice its presence. . . .

He was walking with a measured step, believing that thus he would give more tranquility and method to his thinking. We had been moving along this way for a very long time. But the earth was sounding beneath our footsteps without our hearing it.[1] And the sun was sinking very low without our noticing it.

Suddenly he spoke, letting his sentences drag, and looking at the ground:

"You see, the unity that I am searching for in my mind does not exist. But I believe that the very principle of the unity of this thought lies in the fact of not having any. I would rather not make paradoxes, but I say what I feel very deeply. Or, rather, no," he continued, "I was not thinking this out very deeply. And I thought I could persuade myself with words. But for once I want to be honest with myself. In truth, I believe in unity. And I believe in many things."

He looked at me and I saw on his face the silly smile of those who find their discoveries[2] embarrassing. I did not answer. And, believing this a sign of disapproval, he said[3] again:

"You could[4] help me. . . ."

A gesture from me put an end to this attempt at flattery. The gesture cost me a lot.

And he fell again into his silence. I searched the air for the scent of mystery that falls at night upon the fields. He was looking at the sky. One could see too far out across the field. And the night that was approaching separated each thing, bringing it so vividly to life that we stopped.[1]

He spoke again and his voice was veiled:

"I have suffered a lot. And these spectacles that used to fill me with calmness and serenity only arouse in me the lassitude of old sadness. I no longer hope for the future. I do not believe in myself any longer. I no longer know how to nourish myself on my past. As for my present . . ."

He had said this very simply without any gesture; I was going to say, without any voice, so colorless was his voice. And because this human being seemed no longer to participate in an anguish so detached from him, it seemed more frightening and more inexorable.

And I, who was barely beginning to practice negation, was very moved. A skeptical smile appeared on my lips.

He saw it. But he understood. And for the first time this very old man, who had suffered very much, seemed important to me and worthy of love.

We came back afterward through the night that had now fallen. The barking of a dog made a hole in the silence. And we felt very close to one another. He was not speaking any more now. As for myself, I had a lot to say. But I was silent. I was annoyed that there were stars.

When we arrived in front of his house, he stopped. I could only see his silhouette and the wide-brimmed[2] hat on which I focused. He had taken my hand and I felt his very old skin beneath my fingers. At least I thought it was old and I would not have known how to say why. I loved him for his suffering and because he was ridiculous. But I was embarrassed by his silence.

And for the first time I spoke. And very quickly I, in turn, told all that I had hidden of my hopes and desires for the infinite. I had the feeling I was unburdening myself. I also had the vague feeling that I owed him this confession.

When I had finished, a new silence hovered. Then slowly he drew me toward him and placed a kiss[1] on my forehead. The door of the house clicked shut. I was alone.

And I left again slowly, calmed a bit, in the enormous silence. I believe I felt like weeping, but I remember that the thought that this man was going to die soon restored some strength to me.

4. Desire

He said to me one day, however:

"How I should like to love life! I should like to rid myself of all constraint. I am afraid of death. It blinds me. I am content to wait. It is sad to touch an end. Also, I do not want to love life. It is something too close and too tangible. I would reach it immediately."

We were strolling in the town and his choppy sentences helped me to understand my confusion and my own sudden changes.

"The truth," said I, "is that you believe in something higher."

"The truth," said he, "is that I am trying to believe."

Suddenly this conversation seemed horribly empty and trite to me. Doubtless to him, too, for he buried himself in peevish silence.[1]

The town was noisy about us. But the noises, the lights, and the movement could not make me forget the sky above. Bewildered by this vain agitation, I suddenly had the unexpected intuition that every man, after all, could think[2] and search as I was doing. And this world that I imagined at first confronting me as a whole suddenly seemed to me composed of innumerable elements separated from one another but trying to regroup. So I had the unexpected intuition of a truth. But I tried in vain to recover that fleeting flash of light.

Vanquished,[3] I thought of the innumerable flashes of this sort, scarcely glimpsed and leaving me desperately thirsting for the truth and the ideal.

As for him, he spoke suddenly, as if he were following up on an idea:

"And the prince refused. But he went into the forest, which was singing, and gathered flowers there that the Dream had sown. And, having breathed the perfume of these flowers, he knew the torment of eternal Love."

I understood that he was dreaming of his vain aspirations. But I understood, too, the factitiousness of a pain that wanted to make display of itself. And I grew more and more imbued with the idea that one ought to be silent.

I thought again of sudden intuitions flashing through the night of my uncertainties, and persuaded myself that there alone was truth, where[1] intelligence could not easily enter, but to which only flashes of almost material lucidity permitted access. I persuaded myself easily, too, that the intelligence we generally consider as clear and methodical is only an obscure and tortuous labyrinth compared to these immediate presciences.

And he did not understand this. Triumphant, I looked at him. He who once[2] upon a time used to read my thoughts remained alien to my present ruminations. For I had entered very deeply into myself. I[3] had probed myself attentively instead of seeking the truth in appearances. Not that I had reached any sort of result. But the mute satisfaction of having, even for only a few seconds, glimpsed a part of the precious truth, was beginning to combat the despair of having let it escape.

At the corner of a street, he left me. For he was only the "me" that I had become accustomed to watching act[4] beneath my eyes. He disappeared, for I had at last united the spectator and the actor in the same desire for the ideal and the infinite.[5]

And the disappearance gave me good auguries for my future quests. If up to now such hopes have been disappointed, must I conclude that they will always be?

5. Back Again to Myself

One day[6] the fool returned. And I understood from his weary air that he had failed. One cannot forget oneself this way. Only words had been able to assure us of the contrary.[1] . . .

And this defeat immediately persuaded me that the truth that we had recognized together was the good one. This conviction was not arrived at by reasoning. A new intuition had thrust it on me.

And calmed, at last, I said to the fool:

"You[2] are too weak,[3] but this mission you imposed upon yourself, from which I shrank, do not believe it was illusory. Just because you were not up to it, don't think someone else might not have been. Such a person will come one day, stronger in his presciences and his intuitions.[4] He will act without knowing it. You knew what you were attempting. This is why you failed. But that person to come may be you. It might also be me. It would be enough for us to be making progress."

"Yes," he said, "and I was wrong to be scornful of you. Everything must be done again. But the joy of having thought of it[5] is still ours."

Evening was falling. The room was growing dark. I did not turn on any light. But I opened the window and both of us looked out at the street.

Some people were passing by without haste. I felt myself filled with love for them. I loved them because I know in a certain way that their indifference concealed[6] a whole world of expectations and disappointments. I was not different from other men. I realized that the common lot was not so banal. And I told myself that, consumed with useless efforts and torn by a thousand hesitations, my life was beautiful because of these hesitations, since they are so many sufferings.

I was at this point in my reflections when I felt the fool's hand upon mine. And the contact with his hand, reminding me of an external presence, made a new lightning flash and a new prescience surge up in me.

I saw clearly that I was lying to myself. And it was because the lie was a sweet one.

I did not believe what I was thinking. I would not put my decisions into action. For I was thinking and deciding too much. I was trying in vain to find my true thought: there are some truths one discovers suddenly at a detour of the mind and from which one turns away with horror in order not to discover them fully.

The evening air was brisk and the tiresome noises of the town rose up[1] to us.

And the fool said to me:

"Seek in order not to find. Always.[2] For you are much too tormented to abandon the quest. . . . But, you see, we shall at least have found something."

—"What?" said I.

—"Lassitude."

What more shall I say? I am sick of so much seeking.[3] And this evening is too much like other evenings. All of what I have said, I ought to have kept silent about. But my pride is not great enough for that. I am sad from having been stripped so bare. But I love my falsehoods and my expectations too much not to shout[4] them out with fervor.

Where shall I turn? I know one thing only: my mystical soul burning to give itself with enthusiasm, with faith, with fervor.[5]

| 1933 |

Reading
Notes

April, 1933

What one can gain from reading Stendhal: contempt for appearances.

I ought to learn to master my sensitivity, too ready to spill over. I thought I was past master at the art of concealing it beneath irony and coolness. I must come down a few pegs. It is too vivid, too obtrusive, inopportune. It makes me too prone to impressionism, to the immediate, to the facile, to the "fatal." Through it, I take delight in insignificant languor.

My sensitivity ought to speak, not shout. One ought, since I want to write, to be able to feel it in my work, not in my life.

But is it worth the trouble? I value my contradictions too highly. I dwell too often on consideration of the natural weakness of my character in the grip of an occasional energy which is very real.

My *Moorish House* is finished. It is doubtless better than what I've already shown to G. I forced myself to reveal nothing in it of my present troubles. But I let a little of the pain burst through in the final lines. It ought to be so. Yet I don't conceal from myself that the part where I tried to hide my need to weep is the best.

Have reread Stendhal the whole day. Impossible to work. *The Abbess of Castro* and the *Italian Chronicles*.

They do not move me. They satisfy me. What personal objectivity! An example to propose myself. G. is right.

I am surprised at myself just now for according more importance than it deserves (I realize this very much) to my *Moorish House*. Doubtless it's because of the work it cost me, when I think how small it is in size. I forbid myself to reread it before G. does.

Cursed pride.

Have reread Aeschylus's *Prometheus*. The romanticism of Prometheus. His complacency in misfortune. Bitter satisfaction at injustice. Misunderstood, unappreciated, this makes him proud.

The art of the Byzantine portrait: to give importance to the eyes, enlarging them inordinately . . . so as constantly to remind one of the beyond and the religious impulse. Interesting as a relationship. Why the eyes? Am afraid of the cliché.

When walked across the city with S. C., delighted at reciting poetry and banalities in order to conceal a very natural excitement. The sun smelled good along the quays.

The play of landscapes fleeing from the automobile: the admirable pageants that strike the senses vividly only to vanish in the end, with all the misty magic of memory.

The air pure and clear. The sun perceptible and

ethereal. . . . Lying in the grass. Above my head the
oaks subdue the sun. . . . I close eyes wounded by
this light. The night of eyelids. And the slow feelings
that swell there as if in the shady coolness of closed
rooms. . . .

I cannot imagine Gide loving with an exclusive love.
Perhaps this is what he is tending toward.

I cannot imagine Gide on his deathbed.

The passivity of Gide's attitude.

Have reread my notes on Gide. Frightfully trite.
Childish commonplaces. I became enraged at the
mediocrity of my thinking in view of the depth of
feeling that I have for Gide.

I end up persuading myself that one cannot talk
about people one loves too much.

Surprised by Léon Chestov. Again the adventure
that had gripped me after reading Proust: so many
things to say no longer.

Dostoevsky and Nietzsche, not Chestov: the despair
over ordinary life. This idea carries me along. But I
am scornful of its facileness. It is too natural. Yet, by
deepening it, Chestov seems to make a new idea of
it. Besides, perhaps this idea is not natural to a Rus-
sian such as Chestov.

One might hold that just as there is a need for unity,
there is a need for death, because it permits life to
form a single block, in opposition. To develop and
state precisely.

.   .   .

Have read Grenier's book. He put his whole self in it and I feel the admiration and the love he inspires in me grow. Of him it can be said that he assumes the greatest possible humanity precisely by trying to keep his distance from it. The unity of his book is the constant presence of death. This makes it clear why the very sight of G., though not changing anything about the way I am, makes me graver, more deeply concerned about the gravity of life.

I do not know another man who can do this to me. Two hours spent with him are always enlarging. Will I ever know everything I owe to him?

Have altered the ending of my *Moorish House*, despite what I said about it. I come back to what I said: my sensitivity must speak, not shout.

Isn't it a mistake to confine these notes to my spiritual activity only?

Grenier: "Independence can be nothing else than the free choice of a dependence." Variant: "Freedom from slavery is given in order to be free."

The glib loquacity of the sun.

Art is born of constraints. Let's generalize: life is born of constraints. Restrained feeling ought to be the most flourishing.

What in Gide is called need for justification is the need Gide has to make peace between his lucid being and his passionate being. His lucid being needs the justification of his passionate being.

If there is a need for justification, it is for a justification toward himself. . . .

The Counterfeiters: A writer struggling with Reality, which is opposed to what he wishes to make of it.

The true Gide may well perhaps be André Walter: "I am pure, I am pure, I am pure." In all his work one discovers this frantic need for purity. . . .

It would be good someday to voice some platitudes about Gide, platitudes profoundly true, but as only platitudes can be. Like this: that Gide is only great at platitudes.

Gide's work is a screen in front of his life: "Our books will not have been very truthful accounts of our woes."

When G. loves and speaks passionately, there is always Gide watching Gide. With Gide there is always a dreadful duality between his need for childhood and . . . his ironic lucidity.

Gide is only himself when he understands that this conflict is ours and mythifies it. He understands it often. Hence the pent-up sobs in each of his sentences.

Gide has strived too much for distance from Gide. This is the aspect of Gide I immediately understood.

But isn't this because I am looking for a way to become distant from myself?

And the drama, the suffering of Gide, is to rediscover himself at every step. This is even apparent in his work. In his latest works he has tried to be objective: each landscape, each character is Gidian from whatever perspective it be.

I no longer dare reread *Fruits* [*of the Earth*], in order to keep intact the memory of the rapture and the ecstasy it brought me.

I have never been able to imagine Gide loving with an exclusive love. And yet this is what he is waiting for, what he has waited for.

I cannot imagine Gide on his deathbed.

Fruits of the Earth: this vindication of the senses . . . is never anything but an intellectualization of the senses. There is nothing more intellectual than *Fruits of the Earth*. The very fact of theorizing it annihilated, emasculated that Dionysiac theory. Its truth could not be found except in the very realization of this vicious circle. *Fruits of the Earth:* forbidden Paradise. . . .

The Moorish
House

The restlessness that floats beneath the dome of the entryway, the confused attraction of the blue corridor, amazement at a sudden flowering of light heightening the importance of the brief semi-darkness that leads finally to the patio—infinitely wide, horizontal, perfect with light—these subtle and fleeting emotions that the first visit to a Moorish house produces, I have wanted to enlarge into more general and more human correspondences, in the presence of natural creations. I have wanted to build a house of emotions, Moorish in its design and its desire for escape. Here it is.—In it, blue penumbras and sunny courtyards succeed one another. The same question is posed in the darkness and the light.

At this hour when I no longer have any hope, I have yielded to the vain pride of building it, trusting all the same in the seductiveness of this new dream. I had said to it: "Arrogant, conceited, jealous of the world you enclose, let me forget myself." But from no longer wishing to forget, I hate it now. It will crumble: I was sustaining it on my faith and expectations, now vanished.

The Entrance

I moved forward on the terrace from which the whole Arab town and the sea took one by surprise.

. . . .

The evening is softened by flights of seagulls and, forgetting its violent daytime colors, the city gradually, sadly grows dark. But as the colors slowly become diluted, the brutal movement of the descent toward the sea remains, stubbornly contradicting the hour. The peace that descends from the sky is disturbed by the houses jostling one another right down to the sea, which they run up against abruptly. Their elbowings hollow out streets, blind alleyways, whirls of terraces grimacing insults to the evening calm. Sensitive and beautiful in its impunity, the crowd descending toward the water is very much alive. Its agitation is so real, so human, that one is almost vexed at not hearing any noises. Cries would break the inhuman contrast that thickens and thrives in the silence.

But then one must forget the city and watch the sea, very far away, flat, serene, where tugboats trace great straight lines fanning out in shudders of foam. One must watch it flee boldly toward the first stars, which bare themselves, pure, immodest. Then the calmness of the waters joins that of the skies, while on this side of one's gaze the city strives in vain to disturb the fleeting harmony.

. . . .

When night covered the sky, I went down to the harbor. For a long time I watched the lights of a steamship in the dark waters. My uneasiness returned then, as I watched this primordial mixture of water and light about which one could not have said whether the water was stirring up the light or the light was drowning out the water. Uneasiness, too, before the conflict between two elements. A binary rhythm, excruciating, cruel and despotic jazz, without nostalgia, in the presence of the water and the light, the city and the sky, always.

Like those sexless voices in cathedrals which rise swiftly to the highest vaults while the dark mass of the choir silently accentuates the ardent arrow, like those voices whose supplication strains desperately without faltering toward a final death, like those mystical voices grown drunk on their own mysticism which forget the domes separating them from God, like those stubborn and sustained, avid and ecstatic voices, like those proud laments that one understands only in the sensuality of the Church, like those voices, finally, which do not find in seeking but in giving of themselves, I had dreamed of life.

The Corridor

The immense park cries out in the wind and its intense life rears up at the rain. The irregular sound of the water on the wide leaves rises like a protest along with the stale smell of soaked earth. The enormous silence that had reigned in this public garden before the storm is massed beneath the archway that shelters me. With sullen obstinacy, I watch the rain creating ephemeral elves on the water of the pool or lovingly abandoning itself on the ground. No solitude in this timorous poetry. But it suggests nothing more than a bitter disgust with beauty and the sublime. Gently scented breezes, full of moist earth and mimosa, stir air dense with humidity, and wide acanthus leaves rustle noisily.

Nothing in the garden but the rains and the wind, and the splashing of the water on the leaves and their exasperated rustling. The sharp cry of a blackbird flying off to some shelter further away. Then silence. One perceives each moment that flows by distinctly, and in each moment there is a touch of painful dread of what is going to happen.

For a long, long time, water spatters down upon the arbor. Then all grows calm, the sky still somber. And life begins again, at last, with the despair of the water slowly trickling from wet branches. One waits for the final cracklings of bamboo in the approaching evening. Evening! I think then of the marvelous fabrics hanging at the Arab merchants'. At this hour I see blues and pinks again in the golden shops, then the magic fabrics of silver and silk made more delicate by the light, laughing like children, without reason. And the invariable polychromy of the insolent yellows, the pinks heedless of harmony, the blues forgetful of good taste comes to life for me again intensely like a confused call, a harem made of fabrics like women with incoherent, comfortless ideas. Festive dresses hanging on flat mannequins with knowing, silly smiles.

Leaving the sickening melancholy of this garden, I imagined such a tumult of color taking me by surprise on a rough street, a street I liked because it refused to carry me and only grudgingly permitted itself to be walked upon. Then I stopped in the evening, not knowing where to rest my eyes, dazzled by the gaiety of the color, the vibration of the tones, jarring, jostling, offending, and enchanting my eyes.

And, just as I am now leaving what was for an instant my life, I moved away then from those shops, my eyes filled with warmth.—To dream nonetheless of the sound of water dripping on the silence of an arbor.

The Fall of Light

As in those Arab houses, emerging from a corridor that pursues its semi-darkness in a long blue wake, where one stops, surprised by a sudden fall of light, all feelings and thoughts blocked in a sudden communion, happy because it doesn't doubt it is—emerging thus from myself one day, I had a glimpse, still imprecise, of peace and light, without wondering if here at last was the agonizing happiness I had been seeking with all my strength.

I was prepared for it first by the warm oblivion I enjoyed in the remote courtyard of a museum. The sun was relieving this inner courtyard of all its false sentimentality, which took last refuge in a delicate colonnade. The slightly precious architecture of broken arches and mosaics shrank from the odorous abundance of the sun.

At the four corners of a rectangular pool, vigorous tufts of papyrus stretched avidly toward the light. Bending above the water, one could prolong one's reverie in the pale sea—green transparency of slow green runners at the very bottom.

Wide slabs of stone velvety with warmth invited

one to rest. And one tasted oblivion in a robe of sunshine, living without thinking and above all without
acting, stretched out lazily and absorbed in the unique
sensation of invading warmth. Over all this, one could
see the sky, a proud and spacious blue. There was no
noise, no birdsong, no frog croaking, only the in-
distinct and sleep-inducing hum of the great heat.

Sometimes, just by opening the eyes, one could
perceive leaves and branches, immobile in the arcature
of a window at the end of the court. And the contemplation of this living nature inspired only the instinctive wish to rediscover the previous annihilation.
That day, I accepted the sun. I had an intuition of its
purifying strength, ruinous to false languor and
dreamy insignificance. But afterward a long meander-
ing walk through the city led me into a little Moslem
cemetery. The day was peaceful. A mosque protected
the graveyard under the fig trees. The cradle-shaped
tombs roused no despairing thought, and the inscriptions were reassuring because they were incomprehensible. It was close to noon. From a terrace jutting
forward, one discovered a flight of roofs ending confusedly in the blue of the sea, very far away. And the
sun gently warmed the white and tender air: peace.
There was no one near the graves. It seemed this calm
retreat must satisfy those who were dead. The single
virtue of the silence and the peace was teaching them
indifference now. The eye wandered from the simple
white marble, stained by the fig trees with capricious
shadows, to the curly balustrade, then followed the
rooftops to lose itself in the sea.

It was in this narrow and silent peace, in this infinite

calm and whiteness, that I began to scorn the love of pathos that had guided me too often. Not that there was a lesson in this mute dwelling place: it was content to exist, to live a peaceful and indifferent life, which did not deign to be scornful. It was quite willing to shelter passions and follies, without ceasing to turn itself toward that blue and restful infinity in the delicious fog of faraway.

Along the wall of the mosque ran a gentle shadow the very sight of which was refreshing. And but for that shadow, moving forward little by little and gaining on the graves, one might have thought life was suspended there, that the flow of time had come to a halt. The cemetery was contemplating. There was no weariness in this pause from life, but rightly a plenitude of indifference.

To break the enchantment, there had to be a bird noisily startled in the branches of a fig tree hurling its poetry into this peace.

I went down again toward the city.

Last Penumbra

All houses have their drama. There are two I like. There is the Arab house, which conceals beneath ironic colors the importance of an escape toward the ideal and the infinite. There is also the gray house that masks the capital drama of mediocrity. I love them both for what they seek beneath their indifferent air. Secretive, jealous, they do not want to reveal the ridiculousness of an appeal that spirals toward the infinite. They want very much to be thought gay or indifferent. They don't want people to know. I understand them so well.

I hate them, these arrogant, conceited houses, as I hate myself sometimes for being stupidly proud of suffering and constraint.

And today, emerging from the Moorish house I have just visited, my hatred asks of them as if of me: "Shall we always be able to forget dreamy lullabies for warm, hard, ordinary songs, to flee the pathetic and the extraordinary? Arab house, through which darkness, semi-darkness, and light stream, teach me to be weary."

On the threshold of the house, I watched the night approach. With their great, disorderly handwriting, the bats were beginning to trace their automatic despair upon the sky. Uncertain still, at this empty hour of so rich a day, rising in me I felt disgust at anxieties in flight. At the close of this evening that I had loved too much, I felt aversion. And my youth was hoping for the return of the light, for hours of sunshine that roasts the wheat, from which a scorched savor of too hot bread rises toward the skies, times when the welcome rapture of great heat brings with it complete communion, communion finally in the delicious prostration, in the dizzying and tormented pause, in the vertiginous whir that suggests goodness, pity, generosity. From an excessive fear of affection I persuaded myself that all grandeur was in pausing and in communion. And rage at this defeat finally made me wish to leave behind the adolescent, who believes in his pride, to become the man, arrived, finished, dying with his habits; it made me wish to fear death without complications and without obsession, simply because one *ought* to fear death, to weep no longer, not out of heroism but over the triteness of it, to lie no longer, not out of candor but over the stupidity of it.

And on the threshold of this house, beneath the dome I had come back to, I saw night drowning a delicate world and I forced myself to believe that youth was revolting in me, avid for the prostration it had wished to avoid and for the light of which it had been deprived.

The Patio

> Oswald, in a strange voice:
> "—Mother, give me the sun."
> —Ibsen, *Ghosts*

There are faces closely linked to a whole part of our aspirations with which one communicates so perfectly, from the outset, that it is not possible to think straight confronting them, but only to speak softly, noiselessly, making use of drab worn-out words, which are given a new value again only by a feeling of complicity.

This is how I remember those faces the Algerian countryside knows how to assume under the splashing of the summer sun. I remember the olive trees of Cherchell raising their hairy slenderness in the golden sun, above the flaming, panting earth. I remember deep valleys of the Kabyle, at noon, when the great birds I had loved in the evening were no longer whirling about. From the bottom of these valleys an overwhelming peace rose toward me, and I enjoyed a glorious vertigo as I leaned over to gaze at the burning whiteness of the dried-up stream beds below. I also remember some of those little seaside villages where I attempted to seize perfection by contemplating water of an absolute blue or by drawing in through my eyelids the multicolored dazzle of a sky white with heat. Not a ripple disturbed the sea then, and in truth the least semblance of motion would have been insufferable. Never having loved this land in which I was born, I wonder still whether I will rediscover anywhere else the equivalent of that ecstasy I tasted beneath the sun, which renounces all.

The annihilating rapture, the dizzying warmth, the abundance, the benevolence of that sky endlessly pouring out the torrent of its light—I doubt that I would find them elsewhere. And elsewhere, too, would there be that warm laziness on the terraces of Moorish cafés, where the natives, with eyes half closed, enjoy the intricate symphony of light?

As I relive these moments, a feeling of gratitude sweeps over me. I think that these moments were happy since they were not at all concerned with being happy. I think that after such moments of oblivion a thirst for generosity and pity used to consume me. I knew how to love. I *knew* that so much seeking to know oneself was enough.

In the enjoyment of songs, smiles, and dancing, one forgets morbid sadness and nauseating melancholy; seeing the birds in the islands, studying the glazed transparency of the streams, losing oneself in the

infinite attraction of the sea and its horizon, one forgets
sterile doubts and petty vanities. By meditating, too,
on suffering, ugliness, and poverty, one can preserve
within oneself a horror of all baseness and the pity
one was afraid to show.

This is how, in the presence of my Algerian sky,
I used to perceive the vanity of my anxieties and used
to dream of unknown sufferings. From having wanted
too much to escape from Reality, I learned there is
another unrecognized evasion: forgetting the Dream
in rapture over nature.

And so, in the presence of that abundant light, I
used to feel rising in me along with tears an ardent
prayer that said: "You who have no name, let me
forget myself."

But memories are sterile. It is time to return to
dazzling noons, to pure, harsh colors, it is time to see
again the olive trees at Cherchell, the valleys of
Kabyle, and the little villages that snuggle up against
the waves.

It is time to love and purify oneself in the confused
music of the heat and the sun.

By Way of Conclusion

Slowly, seriously and in forgetfulness, also in earnest
joy, I have built my house. And now seeing it built
stirs regret within me for the secret emotions I
savored, from which it gave me shelter. I grow uneasy
at having to go in search again, since it is finished—
no longer mine.

Before it was created, in the cool darkness of its closed rooms I followed attentively the slow unfolding of feeling that, though vague, still gave me complete joys, indefinable rarities sprung forth in the hothouse of the Dream.

It is built now and I despair at feeling it steal away from me, at seeing it, with an outrageous lucidity, slowly, ineluctably rejoin the abyss where, heedless of the man it used to shelter, it will have for its stucco finish only the misty charm of memory.

Courage

(Fragment)

Five of them lived together: the grandmother, her younger son, her eldest daughter, and the daughter's two children. The son was almost mute; the daughter, an invalid, thought with difficulty, and of the two children one was already working for an insurance company while the younger one pursued his studies. At seventy years of age the grandmother still dominated everybody. Above her bed one could see a portrait of her, five years younger, without a wrinkle, with immense pale, cold eyes, standing straight, in a (black) dress closed at the neck by a silver medal; she had a queenly carriage that she gave up only with age and still attempted to recover when someone greeted her in the street.

It was to those pale transparent eyes that her grandson owed a memory that still made him blush. His grandmother waited until there were visitors to ask him, fixing him with a severe look: "Who do you like better, your mother or your grandmother?" The game grew serious when the mother herself was present, for in every case the child replied: "My grandmother," with a great surge of love in his heart for the mother who was always so peculiarly silent. Or else when visitors expressed surprise at this preference, the mother said: "It's because it is she who raised him." It was also because the grandmother considered love a thing one demands. She drew her rigidity and her intolerance from her awareness of being a good mother. She had never betrayed her husband, had given him nine children, and, after his death, had raised her small family with fortitude. Leaving their little suburban farm, they had fallen into an old working-class neighborhood where they had lived for many years. And certainly she was not lacking in qualities. But to her grandsons, who were at the age of absolute judgments, the woman was an actress.

They treasured a meaningful story told by one of their uncles. On his way to visit his mother-in-law, the uncle had noticed her sitting idly at the window, but she had received him with a cloth in hand and excused herself for continuing her work, complaining of how little time caring for the house left her. And one had to admit that everything was this way. Making her exit from a family discussion, she would faint with great facility. She also suffered from painful vomiting owing to a liver infection. But she observed no discretion in the practice of her illness. Instead of isolating herself, she vomited noisily into the kitchen garbage can. And when she would return to the family, pale, eyes filled with tears from the effort, if anyone begged her to go to bed, she would recall there was the kitchen to do and her role in running the house. "It is I who do everything here."

The children grew used to paying no attention to her vomitings, her "attacks," as she called them, nor to her complaints. One day she went to bed and called for the doctor. To humor her, they had him come. The first day he diagnosed a simple indisposition, the second a cancer of the liver, and the third a serious jaundice. But the younger of the two children persisted in seeing this as a new comedy, some more subtle form of make-believe. He was not worried. The woman had oppressed him too long for his first reaction to be pessimistic. There is a sort of painful courage in the refusal to love and in lucidity. But in feigning illness one can actually feel it: the grandmother carried her dissimulation all the way to death. The last day, with her children about, she delivered herself of her in-testinal fermentations. With simplicity, she looked at her grandson: "You see," she said, "I am farting like a little pig." She died an hour later.

Her grandson was very much aware now that he hadn't understood the thing at all. He could not rid himself of the idea that the last and most monstrous of this woman's playacting had been enacted for him. And, though he wondered about what he was feeling, it did not feel like grief. Only on the day of the burial, when everyone exploded in tears, did he weep, but with the fear of not being sincere and of lying in the presence of death. It was a beautiful winter day, sparkling with sunlight. One could foretell the cold, all spangled with yellow, in the blue of the sky. The cemetery looked down over the city and one could see the beautiful transparent sun falling on the bay, trembling with light like a moist lip. Doesn't all that bring reconciliation? The beautiful truth. . . .

Mediterranean

I

Morning laughs, with all its blue and shining teeth,
    at the empty gaze of windowpanes.
Yellows, greens, and reds, on balconies the curtains
    sway.
Bare-armed young girls are hanging out the wash.
    A man; leaning out a window, telescope in hand.

    Bright morning on enameled sea
    Latin pearl that gleams like lilies:
        Mediterranean.

II

Noon on the immobile, ardent sea:
Accepts me without cries: silence and a smile.
    Latin spirit, Antiquity, o modest veil upon the tor-
    tured cry!
Latin life that knows its limits,
    Reassuring past, oh! Mediterranean!
Voices that were silenced still triumph on your shores,
    Affirmative because they denied you!

    Enormous and so light,
You steady and satisfy and murmur the eternity of
    your minutes.

Oh! Mediterranean! with the miracle of your
   history
Enclosed so completely
In the explosion of your smile.
   Inalienable virgin, at each hour her being is con-
      ceived in beings made already.
   Her life is reborn in our pain.
She flies away! and from what ashes—a luminous
   phoenix!
   Mediterranean! your world is in our measure,
Man is joined to tree and the universe plays out the
   comedy in twos
         In travesty of the Golden Number.
Plenitude springs from the simplicity, immense, un-
   broken,
         Oh! nature which does not make leaps!
From the olive tree to the Mantuan, from the sheep
   to his shepherd, nought but unnamable,
   immobile communion.
Virgil embraces the tree, Melibeus leads to pasture.
         Mediterranean!
Fair blue cradle in which certainty is poised,
So near, oh! so near our hands
That our eyes have caressed it and our fingers have
   forsaken it.

III

To the approaching evening, jacket on shoulder, he
      holds open the door—
Licked at by the reflected flame, the man becomes one

with his happiness and dissolves into the
    darkness.
Thus will these men reenter this earth, certain of
        being prolonged,
        Worn out rather than wearied by the
        happiness of having known.
In the graveyard of the sea there is nothing but
        eternity.
The infinite grows weary there, from funereal
        spindles.
The Latin earth does not tremble.
And like the ember jarring, whirling in
        the immobile mask of a circle.
Unconcerned, the inaccessible rapture of the light
        appears.
        But to its sons, this earth opens its arms
        and makes its flesh of their flesh,
And, satiated, they gorge themselves on the
        secret savor of the transformation—
        slowly savoring it as slowly they discover it.

IV

And soon, still and afterward, the teeth, the blue and
        shining teeth.
Light! Light! man is consummated in it.

Dust of sun, sparkling of weapons,
    Essential principle of bodies and the mind,
By you worlds are polished and made human,
By you we are restored and our pains made noble.

Mediterranean

Oh, antiquity impelling us!
Mediterranean, oh! Mediterranean Sea!
Naked, alone, without secrets, your sons await death.
Death will return them to you, pure at last, pure.

O. 1933

In the Presence
of the Dead

"There! She's dead. Isn't she? I won't see her any more. I love her. She dies. And I do not have the right to speak.

"She is still there. She is still beautiful. But she is dead. Yesterday she moved;[1] she even spoke a little; she threw a bit of herself into life. Yesterday I loved her, I was suffering, I knew she was sick, but I also knew she was alive. Now . . .

"It's true, there it is! I do not have the *right*, I do not have *the right*. I am living, my hand moves. She grows rigid on the table, it's true, but I must not feel sorry for myself: she lives. I am alive, if I suffer. However, I am not suffering. There is no cry. There is something that is crying out: yes, she is dead. I quickly took in[2] the totality of the event. She is dead; that is to say that yesterday living, beloved, she is now without thought. And I cannot love her any more. If something in me grows taut, calls out, it is not to her. Rather it is toward the thought: She is dead.

"She is dead, dead. I must shout, call out, hit someone. Yes, I do have the right to cry out, to be shocked. Because they have killed her for me. And killed me. I loved her. They didn't have the right to take her away from me. Or else they should have taken her completely away. And not left me this body, this stone that is no longer her except because I believe

it to be her, I say it is. Ah!" . . . He slapped the
dead body.[1]

A gesture that annoyed him a bit. What troubled
him in this death was not that she was no longer
there, that this mixture of virtues and faults (grave
ones, he thought) had been annihilated, but rather that
the indiscernible behavior, the strangeness of a smile,
the particular angle from which she saw the world, all
that cruelly defined her in her elusive originality was
extinguished. That, he would never see again. Other
women would bring him the same lie, the same
habitual tenderness. Not one of them would be she.
And her lifeless body lacked precisely that: the secret
perfume of the soul that used to slip into her gestures
and by which he used to recognize her. He wondered
if he had loved her. Loving her was necessary *before*.
Now he had to think about the formalities of burial.

He had to admit it to himself, his sudden despair
now seemed to him a comedy. Yet a moment ago, it
had not. Because it is very difficult to determine what
is false and what is true in each of our actions. He
felt this above all[2] acutely, he who not only lied to
others, but who especially avoided himself, often wall-
ing himself in, irritated by his own presence, embarrassed by his own lucidity. For his was a conceited soul, and he knew it, admitted it to himself
and tried to persuade himself that it provoked[3] in him
an ardent longing for grandeur and pathos. A certain
vagueness in thinking, a complacency that invaded
him in the gray hours of the evenings permitted him

to believe in the infinity of his aspirations. His whole penchant for vague and ill-specified ideas seemed like profundity to him. Yet his ironic self-conceit about all this was bothersome. And his innate pessimism sometimes plunged him into profound disgust with himself, which would have been fine if he had not extended this disgust to humanity as a whole. One must, however, add that he was sensitive to art and knew how to appreciate the beauty of life. He rejected ugliness, loving the strange, and shrinking from the obscure.

His grave faults conferred on him, moreover, a sort of personality. I forgot to mention that he had remained very young.

Now that all was over, there was nothing to do but wait.[1] The burial would take place tomorrow. He thought that he ought to have informed the family, friends, to share the cruel loss that he felt in the person of . . . and so forth (followed by an enumeration of the degrees of relationship usually ending with the words: "and family"). Actually, he did not feel at all like informing the family. They would look at him with curiosity. Despite himself, he would play the game. He would have to shake his head sadly and with an automatic gesture brush away the cruel memory. He would have to be "a broken man." And he felt very much that he wasn't that at all. To be frank about it, he understood all too well that death was darkening a whole corner of the future, which he now saw washed clean as the sky after rain. New aspirations were expanding within him and making him a new and shining soul. Yet he questioned himself uneasily:

he had loved this woman. For her he had even sacrificed some of his dearest preconceptions. He knew, moreover, that the death of this being ought to have driven him to despair. But death had extended itself to the feeling whose object it had annihilated. A feeling of despair—or, rather[1] an explosion of hatred against the soulless body. Therefore a selfish act. So he had not loved her. He had convinced himself that he loved her. If that was what love is, who can say?

He went toward the door. The great vineyards were set out in even rows. The ribbed velvet of the earth was desperately flat, without a tree to disturb the space. It felt good to be alive in the fluid and expanding air. And he looked, with a bit of irony, at the body before him that no longer knew anything of all this.

Losing a
Loved One

Losing a loved one, uncertainty about[1] what we are, these are deprivations that give rise to our worst suffering. We may be idealists, but we need what is tangible. It is by the presence of persons and things that we believe we recognize certainty. And though we may not like it, at least we live with this necessity. But the astonishing or unfortunate thing is that these deprivations bring us the cure at the same time that they give rise to pain. Once we have accepted the fact of loss, we understand that the loved one obstructed a whole corner of the possible, pure now as a sky washed by rain. Freedom emerges from weariness. To be happy is to stop. We are not here in order to stop. Free, we seek anew, enriched by pain. And the perpetual impulse forward always falls back again to gather new strength. The fall is brutal, but we set out again.

When some interest in our life crumbles beneath our feet, we transfer the interest we had accorded it to another possibility, and from this another, and again, without cease. An incessant need to believe, a perpetual projection ahead—such is the necessary comedy, and we shall enact it for a long time. Certain persons even play this pitiable game at the decisive moment. They review their whole life in order to persuade themselves of its nobility. A faint hope animates them: Who knows? the reward . . . or else . . .

But why speak of comedy and games? Nothing of what is lived is a comedy. Our most cynical lies, our basest hypocrisies are worth the respect or the pity due to each living thing. After all, our life may indeed be our work. But if it is necessary to believe that living is nothing but creating, there is a peculiar refinement of cruelty in this gesture that gives rise to what crushes us. It is not easy to believe that without providence[1] to do the bookkeeping of his pain, self-punishing* man furnishes his own despair. And however fanatical he may be, the idealist necessarily forgets his philosophy when his son has died.

But such a man may believe he lost everything with the death of his wife. He realizes that once this misfortune has occurred a new life begins. And even if it should be a life of sorrow or self-denial, the pathos of such an existence still has its attractions. And rightly so; since at any moment it is given to us to be done with it: we are allowed not to live. It can be said of certain people that in any circumstance, happy or not, it is always better for them to die. But from the moment they live, they must accept the ridiculous as well as the sublime. And yet, let us not be mistaken! One can always uncover the ridiculous in the sublime; there are few examples the other way round.

This is why the sorrows we make so much of are, in reality, the least harmful. They are scratches compared to the unfathomable torment for which we believe we live. True pain is not so much to be frustrated over some good thing, but always to aspire

* In the original French text Camus uses the Greek adjective: *héautontimoroumenos*. [E.C.K.]

in vain for the single good thing that tempts us. Doubtless we would not know how to describe it precisely. But the pain that the feeling of its absence gives rise to is the only thing that does not change. It is this pain that reveals its depths to experienced eyes, and about which we say we know nothing in reply to anxious questions. We wish with all our strength for some good thing we know not. And believing ourselves worthy of it makes us misjudge the only ends that we would be able to attain. What's to be done about it? One wave collapses and moans, is covered over by another lamentation, which is drowned beneath the desolation of a third.

And how can I not recall here the Dominican father who told me with great simplicity and in the plainest tone: "When we are in Paradise . . ." There are, then, men who live with such certainty while others seek for it at great cost? I also remember the youth and the gaiety of that father. His serenity had hurt me. In other circumstances it would have estranged me from God. It disturbed me then profoundly. Because doubtless one cannot become estranged from God when it is not he who wishes to keep us apart.

Yes, there are deprivations, there are the deprivations that give rise to our worst sorrows. But what does it truly matter what we lack when what we have is not used up. So many things are susceptible of being loved that surely no discouragement can be final. To know how to suffer, to know how to love, and, when everything collapses, to take everything up once more, simply, the richer from suffering, almost happy from the the awareness of our misery.

God's Dialogue
with His Soul

G: In the end, I'm bored. Because, in point of fact, for thousands of years I have been alone. And it is useless for writers to tell me solitude makes for grandeur; I am not a writer, myself. And I cannot even lie to myself, seeing that I'm at the center of all thought. Me, I am not an idealist. And I don't have the expedience of believing myself damned. The truth is I'm bored. Omniscience, omnipotence, it's always a bit the same thing.

S: Beware, boredom breeds doubt.

G: Say, that's new. You amuse me. That would be quite a farce, wouldn't it? God doubting God. In fact, if I were not sure of being God, the fabulous number of names by which men have called me could one day be lost. Time and Space have arranged to identify me in a good many ways and to attribute me with some horrors I doubtless never committed: Zeus . . . Batara or hunter-center, Jupiter, Zeus or . . . Huitzilopochtli or . . . Ahura Mazda, Indra, and even—what a farce!—Buddha, Ra, Anu or Marduk, Allah, Jehovah, and so many others. Then, as if things were not complicated enough, they advised me to split myself in three. And that makes me think. In all that, which is the real name? As long as it's not Huitzilopochtli. If I could choose, I'd prefer something with a good ring to it.

S: (aside) What a talker!

G: Can't you say something, you? Yes, I know, you're telling yourself I'm getting old. And that, too, makes me uneasy. Suppose this eternity were a lie. Since I can do anything, I can very well have lied. And if I think about it, there are a lot of things about me that might make me doubt. So I know perfectly well that to vanquish me, it is enough for a man to be armed with a good deal of pity. Listen, soul. I'm afraid, I feel doubt insinuating its way into me.

S: . . . (and with good reason, God no longer believed in his soul.)

G: The evil, the doubt that tortures me. Ah! If there were someone above me that I could adore, in whom I could believe. What gets me is not to be able to give myself. There is nothing before me but love. How can I give myself to something that is so inferior to me. Someone above me, for pity's sake! So I can give myself. Alas, I am God. I know very well that there is nothing above me. And I cannot even raise my eyes. Ah! What terrible odors mixed with the smell of grilled flesh. Happy ye who can believe. Happy ye who can give yourselves, can pray, sob, suffer usefully. My suffering can only be useless. Unless I am something else. Perhaps I am not God, am a man like others. Ah! I feel my pride, which hurts at the thought. What to do? What to believe? There is nothing. Ah! I am going to tell men that. I want to see them suffer, too. There is nothing. You should no longer believe. You should no longer hope. I hurl at you the certainty of nothingness. Receive it, make a robe of it, and let the folds fall artfully. And march forward, happy to be the first ones. . . .

But nothing can be done about it. Prometheus gave them blind hope at the same time he gave them fire.

Overwhelmed, God murmured: "My God, I have only one hope. The natives of Tierra del Fuego, at the far end of Patagonia, adore me as a great black man who prohibits evildoing and the killing of little ducklings. If they are right, I am delivered from my misery. The little ducklings will bring me peace."

Contradictions

Accept life, take it as it is? Stupid. The means of doing otherwise? Far from our having to take it, it is life that possesses us and on occasion shuts our mouths.

Accept the human condition? I believe that, on the contrary, revolt is part of human nature.

To pretend to accept what is imposed on us is a sinister comedy. First of all we must live. So many things are capable of being loved that it is ridiculous to seem to desire pain.

Comedy. Pretense. One must be sincere. Sincere at any price, even to our own detriment.

Neither revolt nor despair, moreover. Life with what it has. To accept it or revolt against it is to place oneself in opposition to life. Pure illusion. We are in life. It strikes us, mutilates us, spits in our face. It also illuminates us with crazy and sudden happiness that makes us participants. It is short. That is enough. Still, make no mistake: there is pain. Impossible to evade. Perhaps, deep within ourselves, life's essential lot.

Our contradictions. The mystics and Jesus Christ. Love. Communion. Certainly, but why waste words? More later.

The Hospital
in a Poor
Neighborhood

Millions of little white smiles were descending from
the blue sky. They played on leaves full of rain, in
the puddles, on the moist bottom of the alleyways;
they flew up to the blood-red tiles, and rose swiftly
back toward the lakes of air and sunshine from which
they had overflowed a moment earlier. This made for
great animation, an incessant going and coming from
sky to earth among the hospital wings with red roofs
and white[1] gates.

Like a volley of children from school, a stream of
patients emerged from the tubercular ward. They
were dragging deck chairs behind, which impeded
their steps.[2] They were ugly and bony, and since they
were choking with laughter and coughs, a hubbub rose
from the crowd of them in the tender morning air.
They settled themselves in a circle on a sandy pathway
still moist. Again there was laughter, brief words
exchanged, coughing. For an instant more, then a
sudden silence. There was no longer anything but the
sun. It had rained a great deal on the hospital during
the night, and this May morning was bringing the sun.
They had glimpsed a long swell of it behind the clouds.
Then it had surged forth and, turning in all directions,
had chased the last stormy shadows away. Now it was
lord of the sky.

For a moment the patients surrendered their bodies

to the languor of the air.[1] And resumed their conversation. They laughed in great peals. They laughed at one of their number who did not have all his faculties. He was a former hairdresser: both lungs hollowed out by caverns, the mind foundering in mythomania. To hear him talk, in Paris he had done the hair of the most famous heads in Europe. Gustave V of Sweden had not shown himself proud.[2] And the hairdresser held it as certain that France would prosper under the administration of such a man. But then there were peals of laughter over an astonishing suicide story. Early in his illness, the man had found himself prevented from working, weakened, with no resources, and in despair over the poverty that had settled on his wife and children. He had not been thinking of death, but one day he threw himself beneath the wheels of a passing[3] automobile. "Like that." Only, the driver had braked in time, and in his fury as a man in good health whom someone is trying to annoy, he chased the hairdresser away with a well-placed kick.[4] The hairdresser had not dared consider suicide since.

They laughed. And then they thought: "And Jean Perès, what's become of him?—The fellow from the Gas Company? He's dead. He had only one bad lung. But he wanted to go home. And there he had a wife. And his wife, a horse of a woman! As for him, the sickness had made him like that. He was always after her. She didn't like it, but he was terrible. Well, insisting on it two or three times a day, it ends up killing a sick man." Everyone agreed that by taking precautions one could pull through. Particularly one man, a little shopkeeper,[5] who would say: "Tuberculosis, that's the only illness people know how to cure. Only, it takes time."[1]

Above, a tiny airplane was flying. Its gentle purring floated down to these men. Out in the open air with the fertility of the sky, it seemed that the men's only task was to smile. It felt good to be out. Into these fleshless bodies, reduced to bony lines, came the warm hand of the sun, penetrating deeply, caressing their innermost organs. A spirit floated up from their bodies, perhaps their collective soul, emerging now[2] like some pretty young thing leaving her house with the first rays of the sun.

And one man said: "The illness comes on quickly, but it takes its time to leave."

A silence. They are all looking up at the sky. A voice is raised: "Yes, it's a sickness for the rich." Another yawned: "Ah! Either a little bit sooner or a little bit later."

The airplane was coming back above their raised heads. Looking at it for too long, one grew tired.[3] Now they were in eager discussion. With all their strength, they colored their futures with hope. One had had a temperature of only 100.04° that night instead of 101.03°. Another knew a third-degree tubercular patient who had lived to be seventy. The men lived this way, fearing only their death, hoping on the other hand for a death like everyone else's, a death in some distant future.

A light breeze had sprung up. The olive trees in the garden stirred slowly, revealing their silvery undersides. The great eucalyptus trees with ragged trunks sent their branches to the four corners of the sky. A long bell-ringing. Ten-thirty. Time for lunch. Soon there was nothing in the suddenly deserted garden but the memory of this May morning on which some men, most of them dead now, a few of them cured, had been together.

Art in
Communion

"And I can approve only of those
who seek with lamentation."

—Pascal*

When a young man finds himself at the threshold of
life, on the brink of any undertaking, he often feels
grave weariness and profound disgust at the pettiness
and vanities that have soiled him even as he tried to
deny them; an instinctive aversion rises in him. His
pride revolts at everyday life, which grows even more
humiliating. He doubts: ideas in general, social conventions, everything he has received. A graver matter,
he also doubts the deepest feelings: Faith, Love. He
becomes aware that he is nothing. There he is, alone,
and at a loss. But he knows that he desires, therefore
that he can be something: he must at all cost define
his potentialities. And, besides, he knows the vanity
of what I shall call metaphysical freethinking. From
the harsh contact with inexperience, he thus learns
that his freedom lies in his gifts, and that to obtain
independence is to choose his dependency. His drama:
he must choose. It is God, or Art, or himself. What
does it matter?

And then, only, does the adolescent, who just now
shrank from life, go beyond it and forget it. Thus does
Art rise above life.

* From W. F. Trotter's translation of Pascal's *Pensées*. [E.C.K.]

There is, then, not an opposition between Art and life, but Art's ignorance with regard to life.

Let's stop at this conclusion. How explain it? Actually, Art struggles against death. In seeking to conquer immortality, the artist yields to a vain pride, but a legitimate hope. And this is why Art must remain distant from life and be unaware of it, since life is transitory and mortal. While Art is Pause, life flows rapidly, then is extinguished. What life tries and attempts (in vain, since it cannot turn back to perfect its work), Art realizes. Between life and our awareness, artistic impressions group themselves and assemble to form a sort of screen. A happy prism, when achieved: we have the vague feeling of a deliverance.

Beyond life, beyond its rational limits, Art is found, Communion is found.

And this is true of the individual arts. I believe I can affirm it: Architecture, Painting, Literature, Music. Life comes as well.

I say architecture, although architecture seems, on the other hand, at the service of everyday life. Take, for example, the architecture of an Arab house. It consists generally of a square entryway covered by a dome, then a long corridor that flees into the blue, a sudden fall of light, another smaller corridor at a right angle that leads to the patio, wide, horizontal, and infinite. One can make this architectural device correspond to a sort of affective principle; if one thinks of the restlessness that floats beneath the dome of the entryway, plunging into the uncertain attraction of the blue corridor, illuminated a first time only to rediscover a wandering corridor before it arrives at the infinite truth of the patio, can one not believe that from dome to patio a desire for evasion is developed that responds precisely to the Oriental soul? I don't believe that there is only intellectual subtlety in this. For one cannot deny that the Arab has a wish to create his own personally ordered world, in order to forget the outer one. His house furnishes him with precisely such a world. One specific fact: it is impossible from the outside to perceive anything but the entrance. From the outside of a Moorish house one would not suspect the richness of its internal emotion.

I think at the same time of the medieval cathedrals. It is astonishing to see how their architecture corresponds to symbols and diagrams one might call mystical. Think of the place the triangle has, as a symbol of the trinity and of perfection: the three triangular arrows of the façade, the interior decoration, the stained-glass windows, and so forth.

If I insist on architecture, it's because in this essay I take extreme, at first sight unlikely, examples. Nevertheless I shall end these suggestions about architecture by quoting Plotinus: ". . . The question to ask is how the architect, having adjusted the real house to the internal idea of the house, pronounces that this house is beautiful. It's because the exterior being of the house, if one makes an abstraction of the stones, is only the interior idea, divided according to the exterior mass of the matter and manifesting in multiplicity its indivisible being" [*Ennéades* I, liv. 6, French text].

As for painting, it is easy to show that it creates its own world, true, sometimes more logical: I am thinking of Giotto.

In Giotto's work, churches or houses are purposely smaller than man. The characters are fixed in the silence of a perfect action. On the second level, in front of landscapes that are still conventional,* churches, houses seem like minuscule doll furniture. People have been ingenious at finding explanations: from simple-minded error in perspective to the better-grounded explanation that sees in this bizarreness a consequence of the height at which Giotto's frescoes are set. Yet there is a simpler reason, accepted now, it seems:

Giotto wanted to restore man to his spiritual preeminence, which he symbolized by physical disproportion. All the more so since his characters usually happen to be saints, like Saint Francis of Assisi. One can therefore say that Giotto corrected life, creating a more logical world in which he distributed to each person his true place.

Painting, moreover, furnishes us other examples. Among the moderns, from Impressionism to Cubism by way of Cézanne, there is a logical effort to recreate a special world, very different from the visible reality. Cézanne learned from the Impressionists to see nature with his own eyes and sensibility. He got used to seeing volumes and values rather than lines. And Cubism exaggerated this tendency. The world it creates resembles as little as possible the three-dimensional

* I am thinking of Byzantine art. [A.C.]

world we know. Cubism has been called a "hyper-Cézannism."

I shall treat literature more rapidly. The case of poetry is plain: poetry-prayer, incantation, magic, the mysticism of verse, all has been said. I take only an extreme case of prose, which will not fail to be raised as an objection in such an instance: naturalism. I believe I can assert that naturalism is only worthwhile by what it adds to life. Often it idolizes garbage. Which is then no longer garbage. It is no longer naturalism; it is romanticism. It's a commonplace to see a romantic in Zola. But it is a necessary commonplace.

I arrive at last at music. Music is, from this point of view as from others, the most perfect of the arts. I should like to know what there is in common between a melodic phrase and everyday life. Nothing is more ideal than this art: there is no tangible shape, as in painting and sculpture. And yet each musical work has its own individuality. A sonata, a symphony: they are monuments to the degree a picture or a statue is. Music expresses the perfect in a manner fluid enough and light enough for no effort to be necessary. Music creates life. It also creates death. Think of that admirable passage in *The Divine Comedy* in which Dante, descended into Hell, meets a singer famous in his time. He asks him to sing. At his song, the shadows stop, subjugated, forgetting where they are, where one must "*lasciate ogni speranza.*" And they remain there until their pitiless guards come to fetch them.

Musset was very true and very profound when he

said, as if joking: "It's music that made me believe in God." And one becomes convinced of music's perpetual victory over life in listening to Wagner:

No central point, a uniform and fluid mass forming a whole. A motif attempts to pierce the heart of this mass, feeds itself, fails, and is only complete at the end.* One makes no judgment during the execution: the affective hold is too strong. But when the music is over, when the long plot that the orchestra weaves has slowly unraveled, then only does one perceive that one has tasted oblivion. It is a chaotic mass of shadows, a sensual impersonality, a synthesis, but nothing that is life: an escape from life.

Better yet, if we listen to Bach: his serenity rises without effort, with a single wingspread, above the ordinary. In an art so pure, in a faith so certain, one feels no trembling, unless it is the trembling of perfection, maintained and conserved at each moment by a miracle ceaselessly renewed.

And all music gives us this: Mozart? A divine smile, without lips. Beethoven? According to the Germans' ancient *Edda* mythology, furious and resplendent spirits pass by in the rumbling storm. Chopin? Perfection of the sensibility. Each note stops short of ordinary, silly sentimentality. It is Chopin's grandeur always to run the risk of losing his ideal aristocratic quality and falling back once more into life.

Thus music is the most perfect art. Better than any other, it has shown us Art soaring above life. But all

* *Tristan and Isolde.* Prelude. Love death. [A.C.]

the Arts are identical in a selfsame aspiration: they must ignore life.

Must Art therefore be divine? No. But Art is a means of arriving at the divine. Some might reproach us for lowering Art, by considering it as a means. But means are sometimes more beautiful than ends and the quest more beautiful than the truth. Who has not dreamed of a book or a work of art that would be only a hopeful beginning, profoundly unfinished? There are other means as well besides Art: they are called Faith and Love.

If Paul Claudel is symbolist and realist at the same time, if he is at the same time simple and affected, abstruse and powerful, strong and primitive, he is above all mystic. Claudel understood that man is nothing by himself alone and that he must give himself to something higher. He chose the Christian God. And to this God, he offers what he has: his art, which he raises above the world and transforms into true life, an expression endowed with mysterious and deep meaning, doubtless with mystical intuitions.

These lines offer me an opportunity to bring together in a single piece of work some scattered feelings —wrongly called ideas; to give these feelings a reassuring cohesion. Man needs to assure himself that one can adopt an attitude of logic. Man, with his mania for Unity, bears within himself a need for coherence. Much less a critical study, therefore, than a personal essay, this paper, setting out from Claudel, will doubtless arrive at still broader conclusions, drawn nonetheless from individual instances of Art.

. . .

First of all I spoke of the adolescent's shrinking from life. In Art, always struck by the ugliness of Reality, he falls back on dreaming. But therein, alas! he rediscovers another reality with its beauty and its ugliness. Doubtless this is because through us Dream clings too closely to life. Despite what we do, and by our very existence, we unite these two apparent enemies. And the same disappointments await us in both. The young man understands then that Art is not merely Dream. He persuades himself that he must choose the object for Art from the flow of life and raise it above Space and Time. He understands that Art lies in the Pause, in Communion.

It seems, then, that all plenitude and all grandeur lie in the Pause. The plenitude of a gesture, of a work of art, is only realized if the former and the latter fix, by a limitation, some aspect of the fleeting nature of things in which we take delight. For the dreamy and sterile insignificance of evenings, one must substitute the work of art's more certain light. And what is more pathetic than this pause, since it results from the equilibrium between two powerful forces, since one sees in it the tortured immobility of a too equal struggle—also the delicious fusion of the struggle? One must not seek what lies beneath the delicate world of gesture and form. One must give oneself to it and communicate with it. We are weary of vain quests for the truth: nothing else can come of them but an offensive feeling of uselessness. The peculiar quality of Art is to "fix into eternal formulas what flows in the uncertainty of appearances" (Schopenhauer). Art detaches the object of its contemplation from the rapid flow of phenomena, and that object which, in the dull and uniform current, was only an invisible molecule becomes the infinite Plurality that submerges and overwhelms life.

Conclusion

In rereading these pages, I do not find the desired unity. Doubtless because they are in quest of it. Yet it seems to me I have shown that Art lies in a Communion that ignores life, that I have explained why and made this affirmation specific with some examples.

Nevertheless my essay doesn't seem to me to have achieved certainty. That is because this attempt at definition set out from the spectacle of life and from the disgust it had aroused in the adolescent's soul. In order to arrive at art, it was necessary to turn away from life. And there had to be something from which one could turn in order to make the acquaintance of Art. This is why Art cannot deny life. It postulates it, be it only in contrast. The problem remains whole. Is there no way, then, to resolve it?

The misfortune is that our need for unity always finds itself face to face with dualities whose terms are irreconcilable. A sort of binary rhythm, insistent and despotic, reigns over life and ideas, which may stir up more than lassitude, despair.

But discouragement is not allowed. Weariness and

skepticism are not conclusions. One must go further. One must obstinately dissipate the insistent duality, if need be by an act of faith.

The same adolescent who has led us this far must, confronting what he does not understand, imagine that in him a whole new generation is rising, avid for the destruction it had wished to avoid, and for the light of which it was deprived.

1934

Melusina's Book*

Tale for Some Too Sad Children

It is time to speak of the fairies. In order to escape from the intrepid melancholy of expectation, it is time to create new worlds. Do not believe, though, that fairy tales lie. He who tells them lies—but as soon as it is told, the fairy miracle slowly floats up into the air and goes off to live its life, real, truer than the insolence of everyday. There is nothing left for the storyteller but the bitterness of having given and of having kept nothing. The bitterness or the fervent joy.

One must, then, talk about the fairies. But it is fitting to be selective. For some are boring, because they are too beautiful. And because they are too perfect, some are irritating. The nicest ones, and the closest to us, are still those who are fairies in name only. Weak, unhappy, heedful of anxiety, that is how I should like them. And this means it's impossible to find any. Which means we must create them.

Let's begin by finding the name of the one we settle on. At bottom, this is the most difficult thing. The quest for names or titles supposes great inventive qualities. Which I don't have. Therefore, and in order

* Melusina: a fairy whom the chivalric novels and legends of medieval Poitou, in France, represent as the ancestor and protectress of the noble house of Lusignan. [E.C.K.]

to simplify, I'll call this fairy: She. Furthermore, in fairy tales I very much like to encounter a knight. The knight needs a horse, which we'll call palfrey rather than steed. A matter of music and one's ear. Purely arbitrary. We'll also need a miraculous animal: I would rather have said "mirage-like," again for the ear, but logic deems otherwise. And one has to have a great deal of logic to write a fairy tale. What will this animal be? A bird? Birds have the nasty habit of disturbing the poetry of landscapes with their songs. A dog? Too hackneyed. Better a cat, taking care to remove his boots so as to avoid being commonplace. Perhaps we can now begin our tale. And the plot, you'll say? Unnecessary. A fairy tale ought to set out for adventure without any rules and, insofar as possible, mean nothing. Let's get on with it, then. But I forgot. We must have a woods—that's indispensable.

The fairy is in the woods. She is walking upon flowers that gracefully bend beneath her semblance of weight and lightly unbend to send her on to other flowers. And the fairy proceeds this way, like an insubstantial music, the melodic phrase released from a childlike soul. Just between us, she's a child, this fairy. She doesn't think about the future, or what she's going to have for supper. She lives for her moment and laughs with her flowers. She creates human tales. Doubtless she'd rather like a human to come along, so that with a motion of the hand she could make a few of his wishes come true. I find her more attractive this way, willing to depart from the conventional attitude and let her expectation be understood as serious.

A stream of lively water, precious clarity, something elusive like a rainbow. One could immerse the hands in it and feel the current flow and stop between the fingers. Endlessly dying and instantly reborn. A never-ending miracle, this stream enchants me. For it is the voice of our fairy, who was singing without knowing it, who was singing with her footsteps and the movement of her arms.

Are singing and dancing enough to make a fairy? No. —And if I have shown my fairy in song and dance, I must still show her in more human functions. What good would a fairy be if there were nothing human about her? And song and dance no longer belong to man.

What should our fairy do? If something external does not intervene, she may be occupied with herself alone, directing her mysticism to herself alone. We must therefore have either our knight or our cat intervene.

But the knight is already advancing, beneath my pen, armed with his glory. He is following a path in the same wood. He is upright in his saddle, and the slant of his lance emphasizes his own rigidity. His palfrey—I was right to prefer palfrey to steed: it's a trembling, autumnal noun—his palfrey, then, advances at a steady, curving pace, proud, logical in his gait because he does not know that he is walking. The knight is wearing a helmet with the visor lowered. And since his face cannot be seen, one doesn't know what he is thinking. The advantage in this is that one cannot be mistaken about his feelings. For even in fairy tales faces often lie. Doubtless the soul of this knight is petty and conceited. Otherwise would he take pride in being alone? I mean by "petty and conceited" that it is a wise man's soul. Furthermore, isn't the wise man condemned to remain isolated?

Frankly, I don't find this knight at all sympathetic. His horse walks along too logically. He holds himself too upright. One feels that he is in possession of the truth, or, what comes to the same thing, that at least he is convinced he is. And what's to be done with a knight who possesses the truth?

Still, I reflect, the knights in fairy tales are all sympathetic ones. But what's to be done since this one decidedly annoys me more and more? Let's leave him on the road in the woods. Instead, let's go look for our cat-who-has-escaped-from-the-commonplace.

The cat meows. Nothing extraordinary up to now. But he meows without feeling: you can pretty well see we're in a fairy tale.

He meows for no reason, the way you bite your nails. Proof of his sensitivity. Perhaps he's a romantic cat? Unfortunately, he is an escapee from his usual background, a gutter below an arrogant smokestack, or a crescent-shaped moon in a cloudy sky.

But, actually, where is he? In my brain, says Baudelaire. Baudelaire is wrong. The logic of fairy tales does not permit cats to go promenading in brains. Our cat's situation is more natural; he wants nothing and would like to want something. Which means that all the same he feels the want of something. Furthermore, isn't it very difficult to know what animals think? And only conceit, that companion of knowledge, permits one to decree man's superiority to any animal-machine. In this dispute, it is true, it's all a matter of power. Man is, if not the strongest, the most powerful of the beings. An enemy of fairy tales, he therefore declares not that he doesn't understand the way other creatures live, but that the way they live is inferior and mechanical. But imagine if toads showed themselves the most powerful, and constructed a batrachian civilization; a Cartesian today would soon construct a theory about automaton-man. An affirmation that seems about as convincing to me as that of our tedious genius.

This is to demonstrate the danger there would be in giving too small a place to the cat in our tale. Let us respect this animal in consideration of a future reign by cats. This cat which meows without passion therefore wants nothing. He has rather an obscure need, moreover, a desire for anonymity: "to be the cat which passes by and which must have at least a million original ideas." Actually, I forgot to say that this cat lives in a concierge's lodge on a windowsill, rolled up around his melancholy, with a roving eye and well-kept fur. I had merely indicated that he had lost his lunary and tectal background. But this is because I have a tendency to describe things negatively.

And it's out of pity for this bored domesticated cat that I transported it into my fairy tale. What handsomer escape could he dream of than this venture into a world that any cat, perhaps unknowingly, carries in his oblong pupils? All the more because our fairy tale brings together young characters only. No wicked old hunchbacked hag. Nothing, then, that might remind him of his former mistress, the concierge.

The atrophied tiger enters our story by means of a long, bare, arid, desolated road, not paved with gold: a road to Damascus. Naturally the road leads to the wood within which the tale will be played out. And the cat makes his way in the ditch that runs alongside the road, for cats are loath to walk in the middle.

Watching him proceeding along with his sharp step, I see that he is becoming aware of his new role and that he is beginning to adapt himself to the new atmosphere that surrounds him. His step becomes more fluid, the line of his movement more subtle. With just a bit more will power, he will be merely the essence of a cat.

He continues on his way. He knows that a fairy is in the woods; one can see its first leaves, very high, lurching in the distance. He continues on his way, carrying his offering of vigorous hopes, just recently sprung forth in a world so new. He proceeds, bearing his burden of hopes, heavy with disappointments to come. Cheerful and vibrant, shiny as a brand-new penny, his soul polished and free of its habitual ruts, he makes his way, without acknowledging the person who opens the doors to this brand-new world for him. But cats are ignorant of gratitude. One thing is much more important to them: giving themselves a bath. That's enough to make me love them.

Confronted with my three characters, I am faced with the question of making them act.

The knight continues to make his way across the woods. The cat makes a beeline toward the fairy. The fairy dances alone in the clearing. Isn't she at a disadvantage if the anticipation is richer than the event and the means more certain than the ends?

The knight has reached a crossroads. A little pathway winds its way toward the flowers and the fairy. A great pretentious road leads toward the sky, very far away, where the woods emerge. The knight's fate will be decided here. Will he go toward the fairy or in the direction of the sky? But already his palfrey is moving out onto that grand highway[1] which alone affords the proper setting for its proud gait. And the knight can continue on his way without lowering his lance, as he would have had to on the little garden path to avoid the low-hanging branches.

You can very well see that this knight is not sympathetic at all. He came into our tale armed with pride. He leaves, certain of his truth. Didn't I say so: there's nothing to be done with a knight who's in possession of the truth. Farewell, good knight, and may you one day doubt and suffer. Much will be pardoned you on that day, and perhaps you will be permitted to live out your life in a beautiful fairy tale.

The cat and his hopes are still progressing along their way. He has forgotten home and boredom. He waits, he fears, he hopes. He lives. What does the road's insidious and hardly miraculous dust matter if, over there, the forest is smiling at the fairy's song. Supple and alert, he goes his way. He is happy, for he is expecting happiness. I like him to be happy without knowing it. I should like him always thus. And since I wish it, with each step he takes,[1] the distant foliage falls back in the same proportion. And without ever knowing it, our cat will live eternally in expectation and in fear. He will never reach the fairy; for how could he achieve her better than in anticipation?

I am delighted to give the cat so much. When his tale is done, the cat will move along and always be joyful just the same. He will possess[2] the truth because he will be looking for it. I am happy since I, too, can only approve of those who seek with lamentation.

But our fairy? She does not sing. She is not dancing any longer. Evening has crept beneath the branches. At this doubtful hour the fairy rocks herself. Immensely happy, she is living out her final moments. In a little while the night will make off with her, for fairies, like little girls, may not be out in the evening. Clothed in the anguish of what is going to happen, my fairy is even more beautiful. In the drowsy night the fairy grows larger, larger, swept up into mist, an undulating memory. Her voice is silenced. But the miracle of her death ceaselessly being born again lies in the perfume of the hour. How dark it is! Doubtless it's because my tale is over. Nothing remains for the teller of the tale but the bitterness of having given and of having kept nothing. The bitterness or the fervent joy.

Fairy tales, children's silences, oh! my realities, the only true, the only great ones, I should like to forget myself. Melusina, Morgana, Urgela, Vivian, fairies all, I am thirsty for your humanity. For I, too, wait, I seek, I hope, and do not want to find anything. Having no truth, I do not like great highways. But I like dry roads, sprinkled with hope. The dust of roads, the roughness of ditches are so much rapture for one who knows how to wait.

Happiness from suffering, pride of constraint, oh! my realities, children's silences, fairy tales.

The Fairy's Dream

I know the world's beautiful secret.

.   .   .   .

Melusina floats in her unreality. The gauze of her dress is made of inviolable ignorance and a secret air. And alone, ignored, true but alone, without hope of return, Melusina creates her life and her world through her Dream. This is a fairy's profession.

Without link, without reason, strange images pass by that she frames into the unity of a dream. Melusina the unknown will become revealed. Her pure essential solitude sings and manifests itself, gives itself solely for the pleasure of giving. Behold. Here is Melusina revealed.

Scarcely known, she does not cease admiring herself and here already the world unfolds with variegated flowers and insects, a too beautiful world, unknown because ill seen, above all ill loved. Unreal and true become real, Melusina enjoys the secret taste of this transformation, savoring it slowly because she is discovering it. Orderly, yielding at last, the music of the Dream continues. And what does the fairy's Dream matter to us since it is our reality? It rises gradually in tiers: Melusina is revealed, then pure love and the earth, the air and the water—the beloved animals, proud, adorable, and impudent. Existence springs from the dream, but Melusina lives less and less within it. Melusina conceals herself beneath the joy of the music, the love, and the colors, slowly diminishing, knowing herself less and less. The Dream continues, slowly bowing to adore the earth. The world is still springing forth. An unreal genesis of which Melusina is the verb. Why did she dream our reality?

Unworthy, impure, he who tells the tale in order to speak of Melusina finally springs from the Dream, the only means of coming close to her. Everything continues. Melusina floats now in our reality.

Then everything comes back, everything turns back into gloomy despair and timid revolt. Melusina is weary. The one who tells the tale returns to the air and the earth and the water. And into love, the water, the whole universe, with the flowers, columbines, aconites, jonquils. And even so, love, yawning at the revealed Melusina, in his turn will fall asleep in Melusina.

The Dream grows silent. The effort is vain: there is nothing one can create by dint of loving. Nothing but a caricature. In the world that is disappearing, I remember a trace of silver mist that trailed above a lake, Melusina's robe.

.   .   .   .

That is the world's beautiful secret.

The Boats

There was a child in the clearing, near the pool. Ceaselessly disturbed by a streamlet of water, the basin regained its tranquility along the edges and only there could one meditate on the long green plants, moving but still held fast at their feet by some stubborn enchantment. It was late afternoon. After the sun, the shade was delicious. Moving perfumes that gathered in the little clearing emerged from the surrounding woods. In the still bright sky, as if forgotten, there was a pale moon.

The child had come there to be alone. But a slight uneasiness made his hands awkward and hasty. More than it moved him, the great silence dreaming in the forest frightened him. It seemed false to him, meant to conceal something strange and supernatural. The solitude he had come in search of troubled him now.

It is only at play and by believing that one benefits from being alone.

As for him, desires took hold of him once more. The stream of water before his eyes met the basin without hesitating. From the moss in which it surged forth to the water in which it lost itself, its path went strong and clear. Then the child leaned over and drank, without thirst, this certitude ceaselessly being reborn.

And this was Communion. Divine stagehands lifted the silence. The imprecise harmony rose, affirmed itself, and was the beautiful song of the forest that the child heard, enraptured, anxious, at last alone:

> Que triste et grave est le don, cela, fille
> de ceux que croient, je le connais.
> Fleurs et ruisseaux, dans l'ombre du présent
> tout s'étale et s'enlace, ténèbres et feuillages.
> J'aurais voulu partir mais pour être attaché,
> je vois le ciel trop haut.
> A voir comme les désirs meurent qui regardent en
> arrière, qui donc pourra renaître?
> Non. Non. Que tout s'étonne—de chaque chose
> de chaque naissance et de chaque mort.
> La vie est trop courte qui regrette et désire; hélas!
> je crois à l'Amour, et qu'importent mes racines.
> Je sais que tout arrive et que le communiel
> instant loin de s'attendre se gagne.
> Et lorsque la nuit tombe, c'est l'aube
> qu'il faut atteindre.

That the gift is sad and grave, I know it, child of those who believe.

Flowers and streams, shadows and foliage in the
    dark of the present, all stretch forth and entwine.
I would have liked to leave in order to be bound,
    I see the sky too high.
Seeing how desires that look behind them die,
    who can be born again?
No. No. May all be astonished—at each thing
    at each birth and at each death.
Life with its regrets and desires is too short; alas!
    I believe in Love, and what use are my roots.
I know that everything happens and that the instant
    of communion is not awaited—but is won.
And when night falls, it's dawn
    that one must reach for.

Then the forest grew silent and there, filled with the
hours to come, was a silence gorged on sensuous
pleasure, swooning, until the evening bird, exhausted,
would hurl forth his joy to the stars. Enraptured, the
child knew one must not despair during evening hours.
And, weeping with controlled ecstasy, he threw himself into the forest, to walk toward the edge until the
dawn he had to reach.

The child walks in the night. He has forgotten how the
fertile slopes looked in the light. The woods about
him are becoming enchanted with the promise they
hold. In the clamor of dawn at the very end of night,
love is exiled. But the blackness falls asleep. And the
enraptured hope of love-to-come alone remains. Long
has been the day so filled with regrets, now relin-

quished. The sacred horror of the nights, forgotten, forgotten in the brand-new joy of Love rushing forth to strike.

The forest grows bright with expectation and one can see everything as if there were sun. Here, the traces of hounds, the presage of hastening winter. There, an autumn rustiness, strewn indifferently about.

The child runs, stops, listens. Rain is falling now, fine rain upon the treetops. The leaves are speaking in the splashing forest. The shadows, the wind vanish into holes of night. Ecstatic, the child sets out again and runs toward the calm. Pain, silences, paleness, all that is quite dead. Everything bursts forth now and shines and grows burnished. At last joy approaches, the joy of tables filled with flowers, tables underneath the bowers. Nighttime in the woods. The trees are going to waken. The pine is restless and the oak groans, creaks, sulks. But the child walks on. His path looks out on life. Better, life is in his very path. The child learns about anticipation, sensual pleasure, and what is new. Now he runs along the lake whose daytime belt of flowers he knows, and, in its depths, green shadows, Ophelia's shroud. In the daytime, one must navigate memory's sea-green water where the grasses interfere with progress. Everything encumbered with the past is so long! The child knows that his youth is the truth and that he must hasten to lose it in order to test the voluptuousness of renunciation.

Dawn, dawn finally, full of birds, of aromatic moistures, dawn growing round from the depth of which the child saw his destiny emerging. A destiny serious and dreamy . . .

. . .

Sometimes, often, toward evening, on the trembling water, a timely but surprising flight of boats scatters and slowly moves away toward the horizon.

Timid, evening is scarcely beginning. The boats are erased in the distance and the passion with which one followed them increases with their disappearance. Then the great adventure begins. Then the mind keeps watch and feverishly savors the palpitating, painful, nostalgic questioning.

Thus have I often wished for a tale that was only a beginning and left hanging, deliciously unfinished.

Voices from
the Poor Quarter

To my wife,
December 25, 1934

1

First of all there is the voice of the woman who did
not think.

It is not the memory one should speak of, but the
remembering. For we are in quest neither of past happiness nor of vain consolation. But from those hours
that we bring back from the depths of oblivion, we
preserve above all the unbroken memory of some pure
emotion, some moment that made us participants in
eternity. This alone is true in us. We always know it
too late. These are the hours, the days when we loved,
when we received a sacrament in the bending of a
gesture, the timeliness of a tree in the landscape. And
to recreate the wholeness of that love we have only a
detail, but it suffices: the smell of a bedroom too long
closed; the particular sound of a footstep on the road.
We loved by giving ourselves; finally we were ourselves, since it is only love that restores us. Doubtless
that is why these moments out of the past seem so
fascinating to us. We become aware then of an eternity. And even if it were illusory, we would still greet
it with emotion.

One evening, in the sadness of the hour, in the vague longing occasioned by a sky too gray, too dull, these hours return of their own accord, slowly, as strong, as moving—more exhilarating, perhaps, because of their long journey. In each gesture, we find ourselves again; but it would be futile to believe that this recognition gives rise to anything but sadness. Still, these sadnesses are the most beautiful, for they are hardly aware of themselves. And it is when one feels them coming to an end that one asks for peace and indifference. "The need for peace grows stronger as hope flees, and ends by triumphing over the thirst for life itself" (Conrad). And if we were to speak about these times, it would be a dreamy voice, as if disguised, reciting, speaking inwardly to itself rather than speaking out to others. Perhaps, after all, this is what is called happiness. Running through these memories, we clothe everything in the same discreet garment, and death itself seems to us a backdrop in aged colors, less frightening, almost peaceful. When at last our path stops suddenly before an immediate need, a tenderness unfolds, born of serious reflection about ourselves: we feel our unhappiness and we love the better for it. Yes, perhaps that is happiness, a feeling of compassion for our unhappiness. And the absurdity of this fortuitous tenderness is forgotten when it reviews our past in order to enrich our present.

It was like this on that evening. He was remembering, not a vanished happiness, but a strange feeling that had made him suffer.—He had had a mother. Sometimes she would be asked a question: "What are you thinking about?"—"Nothing," she would answer.—

And it was very true. Everything was there, therefore nothing. Her life, her interests, her children were simply there, with a presence too natural to be felt. She was frail, thought with difficulty. She had a rough and domineering mother, who would have sacrificed everything to a touchy animal pride and who for a long time had dominated the weak mind of her daughter. Emancipated by marriage, the daughter came obediently home when her husband died. He had died on the field of honor, as they say. And in a special place, one can see the Croix de Guerre and the military medal framed in gold. The hospital also sent the widow a bit of shell found in his body. The widow kept it. She has felt no grief for a long time. She has forgotten her husband, but still speaks of the father of her children. In order to raise them, she goes out to work and gives her earnings to her mother, who brings the children up with the whip. And when she strikes them too hard, her daughter says: "Don't hit them on the head." Because they are her children, she is fond of them. She loves them with a hidden and impartial love.

Sometimes, on those evenings he was remembering, she would come back from her exhausting work (as a cleaning woman) to find the house empty: the old woman out shopping, the children not yet back from school. She would huddle in a chair, gazing in front of her, eyes wandering off in the dizzy pursuit of a crack along the floor. As the night thickened around her, this mournful silence would seem irredeemably desolate: no one was there to know it.

Yet one of the children suffers over these attitudes

in which his mother doubtless finds her only happiness. If the child comes in then, he sees her thin shape and bony shoulders, and stops, afraid. He is beginning to feel a lot of things. He is scarcely aware of his own existence. But this animal silence makes him want to weep in pain. He feels sorry for his mother; is this the same as loving her? She has never hugged or kissed him, for she wouldn't know how. He stands for a long time watching her. Feeling separate from her, he becomes conscious of his suffering. She does not hear him, for she is deaf.

In a few moments, the old woman will return, life will start up again: the round light cast by the kerosene lamp, the oilcloth, the shouting, the swearing. Meanwhile, the silence marks a pause, a moment of eternity. Vaguely aware of this, the child thinks the surge of feeling in him is love for his mother. And it must be, because after all she is his mother.

But also he wonders what she is thinking of, what she is thinking of just now? Nothing. Outside, the light, the noises; here, silence in the night. The child will grow, will learn. They are bringing him up and will ask him to be grateful, as if that would spare him pain. His mother will always have these silences. And always the child will question himself as well as his mother. He will suffer as he grows. To be a man, that is what counts. His grandmother will die, then his mother, then he.

His mother has given a sudden start because she was afraid. She scolds her son. He looks silly, watching her like that. He should go do his homework. The child has done his homework. He has loved, suffered, relinquished. Today he is in another room, ugly too, and black. He is a man now. Isn't that what counts?

2

Then there is the voice of the man who was born in order to die.

His voice was certainly triumphant when, with eyebrows knit, he waggled a sententious forefinger, saying: "As for me, my father used to give me five francs a week from my wages as pocket money to last me till the following Saturday. Well, I still managed to save a bit on the side.—First of all, when I went to see my fiancée, I would walk four miles through the open country to get there and four miles to get back. Just you listen to me, now, young men just don't know how to amuse themselves any more these days." They were seated about a round table, three young men and the old man. He was telling them about his petty adventures, and his tales were the measure of what he had been: foolish pranks blown out of proportion, incidents of lassitude he celebrated as victories. He left no silences as he told a story, always in a hurry to get it all out before he was left alone, and he would recall from his past not so much what had really struck him as what he thought would entertain his audience. Making people listen was his only vice, and he refused to notice the ironic looks and sudden mockery that greeted him. To others he was just the typical old man who had grown up, of course, in a time when everything was marvelous. Yet he thought himself the respected elder whose experience carried weight. The young do not know that experience is a defeat and that one must lose everything in order to know a little. He had suffered. He said nothing about that, believing he gained in stature by seeming happy. And even if he was wrong about that, he would have been still more misguided if he had wanted to move people by his unhappiness. How important are an old man's sufferings when life occupies the whole of your being?

He talked, talked, deliciously losing his way in the grayness of his muffled voice. But it could not last. His pleasure called for an ending and the attention of his listeners was waning. He was not even funny any more; he was old. And the young like billiards and cards, a change from the imbecilic work they do every day.

He was soon alone, despite all his efforts and the embroideries to make his story more attractive. Without consideration, the young had left. Alone once more. No longer to be listened to: that's what's terrible when one is old. They condemned him to silence and to solitude. Which meant he was going to die soon. And an old man who is going to die is useless, even annoying, and insidious. He should go away. Unless he holds his tongue: that's the least he could do. And he suffers because he cannot be silent without thinking that he is old.

He got up, however, and left, smiling at everyone about him. But he met only indifferent-looking faces or faces stirred with a gaiety in which he had no right to participate. And with his slow step, the small step of a laboring donkey, he trotted along the sidewalk full of people.

He felt ill and did not want to go home. Usually he was quite happy to get home to his table and the oil lamp, the plates about which his fingers automatically found their places. He still liked to eat his supper in silence, the old woman on the other side of the table, chewing over each mouthful, with an empty head, eyes fixed and dead. This evening he would arrive home later. Supper would have been served and gone cold, his wife would be in bed, not worrying about him, since she knew that he often came home unexpectedly late. She would say, "He's in the moon again," and that would be that.

Now he was walking along with his gently insistent step. He was alone and old. At the end of a life, old age wells up in waves of nausea. It's not much fun on this treadmill one cannot turn back from. Is it that the treadmill keeps moving or is it that everything comes down to not being listened to any longer? Why don't people want to hear him? It would be so easy to deceive him. A smile would be enough, a kindness.

Night is there, descending without hesitation, inevitably: And everything is inevitable for this poor and old man. He walks along silently, turns at the corner of a street, stumbles, and nearly falls. I saw him. It's ridiculous but what can you do about it? After all, he prefers being in the street, being out rather than at home, where for hours on end fever masks the old woman from him and isolates him in his room.

Then, sometimes, the door slowly opens and gapes ajar for an instant. A man comes in, tall, dressed in a light-colored suit. He sits down facing the old man and the minutes pass while he says nothing. He is motionless, just like the door that stood ajar a moment ago. From time to time he strokes his hair and sighs gently. When he has watched the old man for a long time with the same heavy sadness in his eyes, he leaves, silently. The latch clicks behind him and the old man is left, horrified, with an acid, painful fear in his stomach.

Out in the street, however few people he may meet, he is never alone. No doubt he is sick. Perhaps he will fall soon. I'm sure of it.—That will be the end.

His fever sings. His short step hurries: tomorrow everything will be different, tomorrow. Suddenly he realizes that tomorrow will be the same, and the day after tomorrow, and all the other days. And this irremediable discovery overwhelms him. It is ideas like this that kill you. Men kill themselves because they cannot bear such thoughts. Or if they are young, they turn them into epigrams.

Old, mad, drunk, nobody knows. His will be a worthy end, tear-stained, admirable. He will die in beauty, I mean in suffering. That will be a consolation for him. And besides, where can he go? He is old forever.

Now the streets were darker and less populated. Voices were still passing by. In the strange peacefulness of the evening they were becoming more solemn. Behind the hills that encircled the city, there were still some glimmers of daylight. From somewhere out of sight, smoke rose, imposingly, behind the wooded hilltops. It rose slowly in the sky, in tiers, like the branches of a pine tree. The old man closed his eyes. All this belonged to him . . . and to others. As life carried away the rumblings of the town, beneath the foolish, indifferent smile of the sky, he was alone, forsaken, naked, dead already.

Need I describe the other side of this fine coin? Doubtless, in a dark and dirty room, the old woman was laying the table. When dinner was ready, she sat down, looked at the clock, waited a little longer, and then began to eat a hearty meal. She thought to herself: "He's in the moon." That would be that.

3

And then there is the voice that was roused by music.

Just as, when one has been meditating for a long time on the noise of a street, and after the window is closed and silence takes over, men's agitation seems empty of meaning and their gestures ridiculous, almost falling into the void, so did the voice of this woman lose all power and reality when the music that underlined it ceased. Again, just as one did not know what noise was disturbing the street before closing the window and only suffers from the tumult once shrouded in the silence of the room, so the grandeur of this woman seemed routine to those who were listening to her, but later seemed illusory.

The woman was telling her children about her misfortunes. Some music was on when she came in. A record was playing. The ballad was well known but interpreted in an original manner by a whistler and an orchestra. It was called "The Song of the Nightingale." It drew its pathos from its silliness, infused with the sentimentality of a young man who has not yet known life. There was a single theme, which passed from the orchestra to the violin and from the violin to the whistler. Again and again the phrase began, languid and vague, stumbled, whimpered, and finally took up its calvary once more, swelling through the entire orchestra, spelled out by the violin and insinuated by the whistler. Into this immense and senseless melancholy the woman was unburdening her pain. And she talked.

Her unhappiness left no doubt. She lived with her brother, who was deaf, mute, nasty, and stupid. It was of course out of pity that she lived with him. It was also out of fear. If only he had let her live as she pleased! But he prevented her from seeing the man she loved. Yet at their age, this was no longer of great importance. The one she loved also had encumbrances. He was married. The woman who bore his name had been a drunkard for years and didn't tend to her duties. He had a clumsy tenderness for what was exceptional in his life. He brought his lady friend flowers he picked from shrubs in the suburbs, oranges, and liqueurs he won at the fair. Certainly he was not handsome. But beauty is as beauty does and he was so good. For her, too, this was Adventure. She cared for the person who cared about her. Is love anything but this? She did his laundry and tried to do it right. He wore his handkerchiefs folded in a triangle and tied about his neck. She got his handkerchiefs very white and it was one of her joys.

But the other man, her brother, did not want her to receive her friend's visits. She had to see him in secret. She had had a visit from him today. They had been surprised and there had been a terrible row. The handkerchief folded in a triangle was left behind in a dusty corner of the room when they left, and she had come to her son's house to cry.

Truly, what could she do? Her unhappiness was unmistakable. She was too afraid of her brother to leave him. She hated him too much to forget him. He would kill her one day, this was quite certain.

She had said all this in a dejected voice. Now the voice permitted one to guess at the tears that this woman, feeling her abandonment more and more acutely, offered up for those wounds with which God adorns his chosen, and her voice sounded pure because it was hollow.

The music was still playing. The melody came in great heart-rending surges, sweeping the woman's soul along in great gasps. The music rose toward the sky, assailing the divinity so endlessly hoped for. One could feel the Woman growing larger. She bore her tears and offered them up. Without knowing it, she touched happiness. The tune hesitated, exploded with the whole orchestra. And then everything grew calm. After a pause, the violin began again and the Woman's voice grew softer. She said: "What can I do? One of these days I'll end up taking poison. At least I'll have peace."

And those who were listening to her were moved,

not by the words she spoke, but because she uttered them to the accompaniment of the music. (From this intimacy with misery, they felt close to God. And the music spelled out the god to whom they felt so close.) The Woman was not weeping or complaining. She seemed very distant. Her decision had calmed her. Doubtless she would never commit such an act. But having come to this—believing herself capable of suicide, becoming aware that her unhappiness was important enough to give her such ideas—calmed her. Since, after all, there was a way out.

The Woman has got up. There is nothing distant in her expression any longer. But the red eyes, the deep circles, the mouth still out of shape, the parchment-like skin remain. Just as evening brings unexpected gravity and nobility to the most devastated landscapes, her face was made more delicate by tears, by pain overflowing the useless boundary of her features to create a halo about each wrinkle and each sag. Some unknown thing she bears within flows forth from her body to join other bodies, the world—something resembling music or a voice that would tell the truth. It is like a face one contemplates in a mirror, which seems altered, purified, more divine, I mean strange.

She is about to leave. Her hat is stuck on awkwardly, like her smile now. She will come back, she says. She has known adventure, which brought about her unhappiness. The sight of this creature of God's, this ugly, bony body, without the least grace about it, is enough to make one weep. For the God who created her is the God who abandons her, and she knows nothing. She does not think. What, then, is her secret on this earth? But everything is fine, just fine. Let her go away now.

They put the tune back on again after she left. And what will become of her, going off with her fear? She does not exist any longer, since she is no longer there. And yet she must be walking, breathing, taking streets she knows the names of, on her way back to the nasty brutish brother who is waiting for her. She is going back into her darkness, after having briefly emerged because of the miracle of a stupid tune. Her life is slipping away from us and her voice is getting lost, is extinguished already, plunging us into ignorance and masking a corner of the world from us. Like a window closing off the noises from the street.

4

Then there is the voice of the sick old woman left behind by people going to the movies.

She was suffering from an illness she had thought would kill her. The whole of her right side had been paralyzed. Only half of her was in this world, while the other was already foreign to her. This bustling, chattering little old lady, who had lived alone for years, had been reduced to silence and immobility. They had laid her out in an armchair at her daughter's house. She had held fast to her independence, and at the age of seventy still worked to keep it. Now she lived at her daughter's expense.

Alone for long days at a time, illiterate, not very sensitive, her larval life looked out through one window only: God. She believed in him. And the proof is that she has a rosary, a lead statue of Christ, and a stucco one of Saint Joseph carrying the infant Jesus. She doubted her illness was incurable, but said it was so that people would pay attention to her, relying for everything else on the God she loved so badly.

At this moment someone was interested in her. It was a tall pale young man who had feelings. He believed that there was a truth and knew moreover that this woman was going to die, without bothering to resolve the contradiction. He had taken a genuine interest in the old woman's boredom. She had really felt it. And his interest was an unexpected godsend to the invalid. She was eager to tell him her troubles: she was at the end of her tether. And you had to make way for the rising generation. Did she get bored? Of course she did. No one spoke to her. She was in her corner, like a dog. Better to be done with it once and for all. She would sooner die than be a burden on anyone.

Her voice had taken on a quarrelsome note, like someone haggling over a bargain. Still, the young man understood, because he had feelings. Nonetheless, he thought being a burden on others was better than dying. Which proved only one thing: that doubtless he had never been a burden to anyone, except God. And of course he told the old lady—because he had seen the rosary: "You still have God." It was true. But even here she had her troubles. If she happened to spend rather a long time in prayer, if her eyes strayed and followed a pattern in the wallpaper, her daughter would say: "There she is, praying again!"—"What business is that of yours?" the invalid would say. "It's none of my business, but eventually it gets on my nerves." And the old woman would fall silent and close her eyes.

The young man listened to all this with an immense, unfamiliar pain that hurt his chest. And the old woman went on: "She'll see when she is old. She'll need it, too."

It was an obscure and interesting destiny, the old lady's, bereft of everything except God, wholly abandoned to this final illness, virtuous by necessity, too easily convinced that what was left to her was the only thing worth loving, finally and irrevocably immersed in the wretchedness of man in the form of God. The misfortune is that these too equable beliefs scarcely hold up against the first slap of life. And what follows will show that God has no strength against the interests of man.

They had sat down at table. The tall pale young man had been invited to dinner. Because the evening meal is a heavy one, the old lady was not eating. She had stayed in her corner, sitting behind the young man who had been listening to her. And because he felt he was being watched, he couldn't eat very much. Nevertheless, the dinner progressed. Enjoying themselves together, they decided to extend the party by going to the movies. As it happened, a funny film was playing. The young man had blithely accepted, without thinking of the person who continued to exist behind his back, whatever he might be feeling.

They had got up to go wash their hands before

going out. There was obviously no question of the old lady's going, too. Even if she hadn't been half paralyzed, she was too ignorant to be able to understand the film. She said she didn't like the movies. The truth was she couldn't understand them. In any case she was in her corner, vacantly absorbed in her rosary beads. God was behind the rosary and encouraged her trust. The three objects that she kept marked for her the material point where the divine began. Beyond and behind the rosary, the statue of Christ, or of Saint Joseph opened a vast, deep blackness where there was God.

Everyone was ready. They went up to the old lady to kiss her and wish her a good night. She had already understood what was going to happen and was clutching her rosary tightly in her hand. But it was plain the gesture showed as much despair as zeal. Everyone else had kissed her. Only the tall pale young man was left. He had already given her an affectionate handshake and was turning away. But she saw the one person who had taken an interest in her leaving. She did not want to be alone. She could already feel the horror of loneliness, the long, sleepless hours, the deceptive intimacy with God. She was afraid, could not rely on anything any more except man, and, clinging to the one person who had taken an interest in her, held on to his hand, squeezing it, clumsily thanking him in order to justify this insistence. The young man was embarrassed. The others were already turning around to tell him to hurry up. The movie began at nine, and it was better to arrive early so as not to have to wait in line at the box office.

He felt confronted by the most atrocious suffering he had yet known: that of a sick old woman left behind by people going to the movies. He wanted to leave and escape, didn't want to know, tried to draw back his hand. For a moment, he felt an intense hatred for the old woman and thought of slapping her hard across the face.

Finally, he managed to get away, while the invalid, half rising from her armchair, watched with horror as the last certainty in which she could have found rest took its leave. Now there was nothing to protect her. And, abandoned entirely to the thought of her death, she did not know what exactly terrified her, but felt she did not want to be alone. God was of no use to her, except to cut her off from people and leave her in her solitude. She did not want to be without people. So she began to cry.

The others were already outside in the street. The young man who made the mistake of having feelings was gripped with remorse. He looked up at the lighted window, a great dead eye in the silent house. The eye closed. The old woman's daughter said to the pale young man: "She always turns the light off when she's by herself. She likes to sit in the dark."

5

Men build for their old age to come. They want to provide leisure for a time of life beset with irremediable features that leave it without protection. They want to be foremen so they can retire to a little villa.

But as soon as age has overtaken them they realize this is a mistake. They need others for protection.

It is in men that man takes refuge. And the most solitary and anarchistic among them still yearns the most to shine in the eyes of the world. People are what counts. Generations succeed one another, flowing into one another, are born in order to die and be reborn. One day an old woman was in pain? And then? Her destiny is of limited interest only. She, too, takes comfort in man alone. God does little more for her than cut her off from people and leave her in solitude. She does not want that. She weeps.

A man, an old woman, other women have been talking, and slowly, one by one, their voices fade away, muffled into the universal clamor of men, which beats with great throbs like an omnipresent heart.

Notes and
Variants

1932

A New Verlaine

No manuscript. An article published in *Sud*, a magazine of the city of Algiers, March, 1932, p. 38.

Jehan Rictus

No manuscript. An article published in *Sud*, May, 1932.

The Philosophy of the Century

No manuscript. Article published in *Sud*, June, 1932.

Essay on Music

The *Essay on Music* was published in its definitive form in the magazine *Sud*, June, 1932, pp. 123-130. The manuscript takes up twenty-six large pages. Before delivering his text to the printer, Camus made innumerable corrections of detail. Rather than enumerate them all, it seemed preferable to reproduce the draft version of the introduction of the *Essay on Music*, which precedes the section devoted to Schopenhauer:

> To show that music is the most complete and the most perfect of the arts, this is the goal of the present work. It is important beforehand, however, to define clearly the way we conceive of art: According to the realist school, which contrasts in this respect with the idealist school, art ought to concern itself solely and even exclusively with the imitation of nature and the exact reproduction of reality. This definition not only degrades art, it destroys it. To lower it to a servile imitation of nature is to condemn it to reproduce only the imperfect. It must not be forgotten that the greatest part of the aesthetic emotion is brought by our personality. The

share of beauty that exists in nature is so weak that one cannot consider it as appreciable. The feeling of beauty that we have before a landscape does not derive from the aesthetic perfection of that landscape. It comes from the fact that this aspect of things is in perfect agreement with instincts, leanings, vague feelings in our awareness. And this is so true that the same landscape seen for too long a time, too often contemplated, ends up by wearying one. This would not happen if it carried its perfection within itself. No matter what we do, the greatest part of the aesthetic emotion is manufactured by our individual selves and Amiel's epigram will always be right: "*A landscape is a state of soul.*"

Besides, if the arts were reduced to the imitation of nature, admitting that certain of them like painting or sculpture arrive at a result, it is materially impossible for others, like architecture and—above all—music, to do the same. Certainly nature possesses its own harmonies, but I do not believe that one can even dream of saying that Beethoven and Wagner simply imitated them. There would be, moreover, no advantage in attempting reproductions forcibly unfaithful to nature in order to create aesthetic emotion. Nature itself would bring to us much more surely a clearer and purer emotion.

We therefore consider this "realist" thesis as indefensible. Furthermore, the results of this attempt could lead us to the same conclusion. Next to undeniable successes like *Madame Bovary*, how many Zolas are there, fallen into the most vulgar obscenity and garbage. I do not truly believe that one can speak of aesthetic emotion in the presence of *Les Rougon-Macquart*.

What, then, will our conception of art consist of? Not absolutely that of the "idealist" school, which, instead of submitting art to nature, rightly contrasts them, but which makes the principal merit of art consist of what the mind adds to nature. This idealist theory is in reality only a moral theory, productive of flat, false, and boring works by dint of wishing to show wholesome, respectable examples destined to be imitated.

For us, art will be neither the expression of the Real nor the expression of a Real embellished to the point of being falsified. It will simply be the expression of the ideal. It will be the creation of a dream world attractive enough to make us forget the world in which we live with all its horrors. And the aesthetic emotion will reside uniquely in the contemplation of this ideal world. It will be the expression of things such as they ought to be for us. And since each person's ideal varies, art will be essentially personal and original. Art should be the key opening doors to a world ordinarily unrecognizable, where everything would be beautiful, perfect, beauty and perfection being defined according to each one of us. Besides, who tells us that this universe is not the only truth?

And it is by basing our argument on this conception of art that we shall try to prove that music, absolutely fulfilling all the conditions of this theory, is the most perfect as well as the most complete of the arts. In this we shall be aided by the thought of Schopenhauer and that of Nietzsche, which is directly derived from the former, despite certain divergences that we will study. The philosopher of the Will being in this matter a disciple of Plato, it is in short upon Plato that we shall rely. The latter's theory is, furthermore, beautiful enough, "artistic" enough, to be considered as the only good one.

We shall first set forth Schopenhauer's theory so as to better understand his influence on Nietzsche's ideas, and we shall accord a larger place to the latter, a place corresponding, moreover, to the place this philosopher reserved for art in his own work. A poet as much as a philosopher, Nietzsche possesses a personality too fascinating to neglect.

From the exposition of these two theories, I shall try to draw some conclusions as to the definition and the value of music in trying to demonstrate music's supremacy over all the other arts.

Eliminated by Camus, on the other hand, are the outline and the bibliography, which, in the manuscript, accompany the text of his *Essay on Music:*

Outline

Introduction

A. Rejection of the realistic theory of Art.
   To lower art to the imitation of nature is to destroy it.
B. The goal of Art is to make us forget the World in which we live in order to project us into the Dream World.
C. This is why music, fully realizing this ideal, is the most perfect art. We are going to try to demonstrate it by relying on Schopenhauer and Nietzsche.

Schopenhauer and Music

A. Rapid summary of Schopenhauer's general theory: the Will.
B. Schopenhauer's art: Knowledge of Ideas.
C. Music: Expression of the Will parallel to the World of Ideas.

Nietzsche and Music

A. Rapid exposé of Nietzsche's general philosophy. Two aspects of his theory on music.
B. Ideas that Schopenhauer carries to extremes: Birth of Tragedy. Apollo. Dionysus. Music is Redemption.
C. Ideas that provoke Schopenhauer: On Music and Thought. Music does not have as its only function its evocation of our feelings.
D. The first of these ideas leads to the defense of Wagner. The second of these ideas leads to criticism of Wagner.

Attempt at a definition inspired by these two philosophers

A. Music is the expression of an unrecognizable Reality. This Reality would be a World parallel to the Real World.
B. Proof of this affirmation:
   Music is capable of being inspired by feelings, whether literary or personal. The contrary is not possible. Irreducibility of the known to the Unknown.

C. Value of Music. It will be a value of Redemption. Music permits us an escape—temporary, perhaps, but real—thanks to the Rapture of the Beautiful.

D. Relationship to the other arts: Music is the most perfect art.

Conclusion

A. I've kept from Nietzsche's theory all that harmonizes with Schopenhauer. I've rejected the rest: why?

B. This is why I believe that Nietzsche was mistaken in his criticism of Wagner.

C. What will the music that ought to please us be like.

Bibliography

Schopenhauer. *The World as Representation and as Will*, Vol. III

Nietzsche. *The Wagner Case*
Nietzsche Versus Wagner
The Birth of Tragedy (consulted)

Pierre Lasserre. *Les Idées de Nietzsche sur la Musique* (*Nietzsche's Ideas on Music*)

H. Lichtenberger. *La Philosophie de Nietzsche* (*Nietzsche's Philosophy*)

Plotinus. *First Ennead*, Treatise VI: *On the Beautiful*, or *On Beauty*.

Various magazine articles, particularly in the *Revue Musicale*.

In revising the *Essay on Music*, Camus sometimes took account of Jean Grenier's opinions. They figure in the margins of the manuscript. Here are the principal ones:

On the *Essay* as a whole: "Review it: tighten, clarify. Omit what may be academic in it." On the "feeling for the Beautiful" analyzed in the first paragraphs: "This raises problems. (1) Plato's plastic Beauty—imitation of the Idea; (2) or Baudelaire's original ugliness—expression of the individual. Must one choose? You choose number 2. Ancient temples, cathedrals, skyscrapers are anonymous. Have you read Le Corbusier and Jeanneret? Add discussion of this objection to conclusion of part B."

On Schopenhauer's philosophy, set forth at the beginning

of "Schopenhauer and Music," p. 133: "A system derived rather from Buddhism. Tantra: thirst for life." On the harmony that appears, p. 133, between the philosopher's thought and the Scriptures: "Specify that it is only on one point that Schopenhauer is in agreement with the Bible. But no salvation for a God." At the end of the exposition of Schopenhauer's general philosophy, p. 136: "We think it is useless to give an exposition of Schopenhauer's philosophy. Too well-known, this philosophy has also been too misunderstood and, above all, too badly interpreted. Although it was merely a single burst of generous idealism, people were quick to accuse it of egoism. We recall, however, that if Nietzsche was strongly inspired by Schopenhauer, he nonetheless brought about a complete reversal of values, beginning all the while from the same point of departure. . . ." On Schopenhauer's notion of music, p. 138: "Well-done analysis. Don't touch it."

On the considerations of Nietzsche's philosophy at the beginning of "Nietzsche and Music," p. 138: "Modify the generalizations on Schopenhauer and Nietzsche. Suppose these writers already slightly known to the reader. Without full explanations, remind of these generalizations, but without rigor and as notations." On Nietzsche's aristocratic ethics, p. 139: "Quite right. It's a heroic optimism related to that of Calderon, Corneille, Claudel (cf. *The Birth of Tragedy*)." On the birth of Greek harmony, in the middle of political struggles, p. 141: "The Italian Renaissance, too, moreover. Vinci emerges from Borgia." On Greek music, conceived as a form of dreaming, p. 141: "Recall this objection in a few words: don't push Greek unreality too far. Do not forget their sense of limits. The rhythm of Greek dances (which survive in Barcelona through the Sardanas). And does Greek music make Nietzsche entirely right? Nietzsche pushes Greece toward India. It's true he does not accept post-Socratic Greece!" On Wagner's music, which Nietzsche defends, pp. 144–5: "If Wagner did not create myths, at least he gave new vigor to ancient myths. One does not create myths as one wishes. Wagner's are stillborn." On the antithesis Camus establishes between "reason" or "technique" and music, p. 142: "No. Example: Bach. Recast so that it won't be thought an attack against technique when it is an attack against Reason. The great misfortune for the artist is to start out with ideas, feelings, rather than end up by suggesting them. What survives in Wagner is that through which he is musician and not thinker. His (pure) music makes us think; and his thought bores us. Primacy of technique (not to be confused with reason)." On the impossibility of literature's suggesting musical images, p. 148: "The poetry of Burns, Shelley, for example? Have you read Heine's *Intermezzo*?" On the purer world to which music gives access, p. 149: "This is true. But you don't make much of a case for the new world in which it makes us live." On the superiority of music, which "does not need to vanquish matter," to the other arts, p. 153: "True, and also superficial. The art that has the least need of matter is writing—and this absence of obstacles is a misfortune for the writer, who risks being mistaken much more than the architect. The musician must take account of the instrument, the acoustics, the performers, and so on. Happy material difficulties. If music is the most spiritual of all the arts, this is not because it has the least material base; it is because it has a mathematical foundation. Are you acquainted with Leibniz's admirable definition: *Musica, exercitium occultum nescientis se numerare animi.* Unconscious arithmetic."

On the *Essay*'s "Conclusion," in which Camus had at first written about Wagner, "Through his subjects, [he] takes us back into a legendary world, the world of the old mythological warrior Germany, or into the world of mystical Brittany": "No. That's phony." On his praise of Wagner, misunderstood by Nietzsche, p. 154: "Correct, but badly expressed. Wagner's music is often very moving, but only his music. Wagner fails in his try at artistic synthesis. There is always a contrast between the libretto and the symphony. A cruel disparity. Siegfried's tawdriness, the stuffed lions, the valkyries of the Salvation Army, and all those saturnalia for monastic institutions!" Apropos of an imprudent formula preceding the diatribe against "musical acrobatics" in the first version of the *Essay*, "It [music] bestows Reason on us, by calling only upon the senses": "Weak point in your composition. Music ought to be based neither on reason nor on the senses. Mistake. Consider that it is not a question of our senses but rather of something obscure that exists within us." On the last two sentences of the first version of the *Essay*, "Music ought to be able to make us forget anything disturbing in our existence and, by permitting us access to a spiritual world, make us scorn the low appetites and the gross instincts that we carry within us. Then alone will music be both the most perfect art and an instrument of redemption and social regeneration."

Intuitions

With the exception of the prologue and *The Will to Lie*, written at the same time, each of the texts Camus brought together under the general title of *Intuitions* is known to us thanks to two manuscripts, A and B, of which the second and more developed has some differences from the first. The definitive version, B, was, of course, the preferred one. As for the *Deliriums*, the manuscript had been typed, at the time of its final revision, up to and including these words: ". . . this morning I have one great wish: to be like everyone."

The variants will be introduced by the number in the printed text that marks the place where they are situated, and preceded by the letter A. The words, parts of sentences, or sentences crossed out in A or in B are shown in brackets. The most important corrections have been chosen.

These manuscripts, all signed and dated October, 1932 (with *The Will to Lie*, the name of the month, vigorously erased, is still unreadable), are made up of loose pages, of a large size, which have not been paginated. The order in which we have chosen to publish the texts of *Intuitions*, in the absence of an indication from the author, seems the most logical. Doesn't it fall to the Fool to impose his presence in the first (*Deliriums*) and the last (*Back Again to Myself*)? Isn't it fitting for *The Will to Lie* to follow *Uncertainty*, which ends precisely on an obsessive repetition of the word "lie"? And isn't it natural enough for the young narrator, after chatting with his companion, the old man (in *The Will to Lie*), to have a dialogue with his double, with himself (*Desire*)?

1. *Deliriums*

page 156
1. A (*In exergum*): Not sympathy, but my call to beings. A. G. (André Gide)
2. A: Listen, friend,

page 157
1. A: [*liberation*]
2. A: [*Not to want to know, to refuse to know is the sign of a liberation.*]
3. A: [*My mind will not be a laboratory, but a recording machine.*]
4. A: Today, I become double voluntarily. But sometimes this happens to me without my being aware of it.
5. A: And if one day you notice me like this, don't be surprised. Don't think me fickle.

page 158
1. A: and I love
2. A: [*and scarcely*]
3. A: I understood
4. A: he was in one of those moments

page 159
1. A: Well, I see
2. A: I know them.
3. A: And what is still stranger is that you love them.
4. A: , these silences that end with high philosophical speculations.

page 160
1. A: to insist on analyzing.
2. A: After all, laughter is perhaps part of Eternal Beauty.
3. A: Bewildered
4. A: I did not have
5. A: And in order to do that, follow me.

page 161
1. A: The earth, the trees, the sky, everything
2. A: Forget yourself in love.

3. A: For I love you as I love everything.
4. A: And
5. A: original
6. A: Oblivion is a generous cordial.
7. A: my brothers, so numerous, forget your weakness, which would like to display itself and which devotes all its strength toward this end.

page 162
1. A: Men, I bring you happiness in oblivion.
2. A: for the very act of refusing to know life he had set death at a distance.
3. A: we shall live in

page 163
1. A: the splendor of the skies and the pungent vigor
2. A: a sentence unreadable beneath the erasures

2. *Uncertainty*
3. A: entered through the [windows] windowpanes.
4. A: took up the flow again
5. A: And in our our respective indifference

page 164
1. A: those who tell themselves they are made neither to command nor to obey.
2. A: without transition

page 165
1. A: for not [*being a spectator*] finding pleasure in
2. A: [*And I smiled at feeling myself*]
3. A: fixedly without stopping

3. *The Will to Lie*
A single manuscript (Ms).

page 166
1. Ms: A sentence begins here that has been scratched out and that remains illegible [*And life was* . . .]
2. Ms: [*of a spiritual sort*]
3. Ms: [*Undertook*]
4. Ms: [*I should like*]

page 167
1. Ms: [*not of a common accord, but because he stopped*]

2. Ms. [*crumpled wings*]
page 168
1. Ms: [*embraced me*]

4. *Desire*
page 169
1. A: complete mutism
2. A: [*each one thought as*]
3. A: [*desperate*]

page 170
1. A: in which
2. A: [*formerly used to see*]
3. A: And instead of searching for the truth in appearance, I
4. A: to watch as a spectator and which acted
5. A: same rejection of intelligence.

5. *Back Again to Myself*
6. A: One day at last

page 171
1. A: assure ourselves of it.
2. A: My brother, you
3. A: I am, too.
4. A: stronger; he will not have known intelligence.
5. A: I think we must content ourselves with living simply.
6. A: beneath their indifference was concealed

page 172
1. A: reached
2. A: Seek. You will not find. I shall not find, either. We shall therefore always be seeking.
3. A: I suffer too much.
4. A: confess
5. A: (the whole last paragraph): Where shall I turn? But there is one thing I know. That is that there is something else. This life is not all. [*And my sudden intuitions are there for*] And I forge my hope with my sudden intuitions. There is the truth. There is the Goal. Besides I should hope for no goal and no departure. But perhaps I ought to take myself away from these too vague things. Perhaps. But what does it matter. Since my infinite is not on earth.

1933

The Moorish House

To write *The Moorish House*, Albert Camus used a school notebook of small size bought at the Ferraris Bookshop, 43 Rue Michelet, in Algiers. The manuscript, without erasures, is dated April, 1933, and signed. It is probably a definitive copy. No draft has been found.

Courage

The manuscript occupies the last four pages of the notebook described above. There are no erasures. *Courage* is accompanied by a brief text (one page) meant to preface a future collection of essays. (*The Wrong Side and the Right Side?*) In Camus's mind, it seems that *Courage* is intended as the last of these essays:

"It bothers people when one is lucid and ironic. You are told: 'It shows you are not good.' I don't see the connection. If I hear someone say to someone: 'I am an immoralist,' I translate: 'I need to give myself an ethic'; or if I hear someone else say: 'The hell with intelligence,' I understand: 'I cannot stand my doubts.' Because it bothers me that people cheat. And the great courage is to accept oneself, with one's contradictions.

"These essays are born of circumstances. One will feel in them, I believe, the wish to reject nothing of those circumstances. It is true that Mediterranean lands are the only ones where I can live, that I love life and light; but it is also true that the tragic aspect of existence obsesses man and that the deepest silence remains associated with it. Between this wrong side and right side of the world and of myself, I refuse to make a choice. If you see a smile on a man's despairing lips, how do you separate the one from the other? There, beneath the mask of contradiction, irony takes on a metaphysical value. But it is a metaphysics in action. And this is why the last essay bears the title: *Courage*."

Mediterranean

The manuscript, property of Jean de Maisonseul, is made up of two large sheets of paper. It is signed and dated October, 1933.

In the Presence of the Dead

The manuscript is in the form of four large sheets of paper, covered with hasty handwriting. Some corrections and one remarkable variant.

page 200
1. MS: living
2. Ms: understood

page 201
1. Ms: He looked at the body without kindness. A thought came to him that made him shiver: his slap had left no trace. Had the body been alive, the blood would have rushed to the places hit. And then, too, the good complexity of a reaction would have sprung up. He went to wash his hands. At the end of his fingers he felt the heavy inertia of the head.
2. Ms: This impossibility
3. Ms: nourished

page 202
1. Ms: They would come to take her away tomorrow

page 203
1. Ms: and still he wondered if he was in despair

Losing a Loved One

The manuscript is made up of three large pieces of paper. There are very few corrections. It is dated October, 1933. It has no title.

page 204
1. Ms: of

page 205
1. Ms: power

God's Dialogue with His Soul

The manuscript consists of two large sheets of paper, covered with a handwriting rather difficult to decipher. No corrections worth noting. Judging from the handwriting, the text seems to have been written in 1933.

Contradictions

A single sheet of paper, large in size, covered with a nervous handwriting. Neither title nor date. From the handwriting, this text would seem to have been written in 1933.

The Hospital in a Poor Neighborhood

There are two manuscripts, A and B, of *The Hospital in a Poor Neighborhood*. B, which is the property of Jean de Maisonseul and dated 1933, gives the definitive version of the story. A few appreciable variants appear.

page 211
1. A: between the wings of the red-roofed hospital with white gates, among the flowers, the leaves, and the birds.
2. A: [*which made them more awkward*]

page 212
1. A: let their bodies sway in the languor of the air.
2. A: One couldn't say that there hadn't been one like that.
3. A: [*I cannot say that I thought of my daughters and the others. But one day I went down the street. An auto went by. I did not think.*]
4. A: [*"He gave me a kick in the pants, I'll only tell you that."*]
5. A: [*a Jew*] made superhuman efforts to reassure himself. They delighted in this.

page 213
1. A: and some precautions.
2. A: [*They felt the infinite happiness of no longer feeling the body's limits. Like a pretty young girl who comes out of her house with the first rays of the sun.*] Like a pretty young girl who leaves her house at the first rays of the sun, their souls emerged now, were floating about their bodies.
3. A: Their heads were growing tired. They no longer cared about the sun.

Art in Communion

The manuscript is made up of eleven large-sized papers. It is signed and dated: "33." The preparation of the text is particularly careful. No correction worth noting.

1934

Melusina's Book

Camus carefully recopied the text of *Melusina's Book* into a small (21 × 17 centimeters), lined school notebook. He did not date it, but Simone Hié [the author's first wife] says she received *Melusina's Book* as a gift during the month of December, 1934.

The variants are few.

Tale for Some Too Sad Children
page 233
1. Ms: pathway

page 234
1. Ms: each step of the cat
2. Ms: nearly
No correction, after this, in *The Fairy's Dream* and *The Boats*.

Voices from
the Poor Quarter

It is possible to reconstitute the ensemble of the text even without recourse to the manuscript copies, which used to belong to Simone Hié. In fact, Roger Quilliot, who made use of the manuscript in his presentation of *The Wrong Side and the Right Side* in the Pléiade edition of Camus's *Essais*, printed, with the owner's permission, all of the unpublished passages or episodes. Here in detail are the elements that were at our disposal in order to establish the text of *Voices from the Poor Quarter*:
1. "The voice of the woman who did not think": *Essais* (Pléiade edition), pp. 1187–1189.
2. "The voice of the man who was born in order to die":

Essais, second part of *Irony,* pp. 17–20, revised thanks to the summary of variants, pp. 1186–1187.

3. "The voice that was roused by music": *Essais,* pp. 1209–1212.

4. "The voice of the sick old woman left behind by people going to the movies": *Essais,* first part of *Irony,* pp. 15–17, revised thanks to the summary of variants, pp. 1185–1187.

5. "Men build for their old age to come": *Essais,* pp. 1212–1213.

Mme. Albert Camus preserves, in addition, a typewritten manuscript of "the voice that was roused by music," two of "the voice of the sick old woman" . . . and two of "the voice of the man who was born in order to die."

Albert Camus had dated *Voices from the Poor Quarter,* dedicating them to his first wife, December 25, 1934.

A Note About the Author

Albert Camus was born in Mondovi, Algeria, in 1913.
In 1939 in Algeria he published a first book
of essays. *The Myth of Sisyphus* and
The Stranger were published in 1942 in occupied
France, bringing him to the attention of intellectual
circles. Among his other major writings are the essay
The Rebel and three widely praised works of fiction,
The Plague, The Fall, and *The Exile and the Kingdom.*
He also published a volume of plays, *Caligula
and Three Other Plays,* as well as various dramatic
adaptations. In 1957 Camus was awarded the
Nobel Prize for Literature. On January 4, 1960, he was
killed in an automobile accident.